PRAISE FOR
THE LAUNCH BOOK

"In *The Launch Book*, Sanyin Siang presents a rich collection of instantly usable advice for readers intent on reaching their full potential. By masterfully curating her own experience with wisdom from an impressive assemblage of industry leaders, Sanyin gives us a wonderfully practical field guide for success."

Keith Reinhard, Chairman Emeritus,
DDB Worldwide and Member, Advertising Hall of Fame

"Too often we don't reveal our true self for fear we are not 'good enough', but for me, *The Launch Book* helps us to unlock our inner-genius and empowers us to remove the mask so that we can launch bravely and successfully."

Jesse J. Tyson, President & CEO, National Black MBA Association and former Head, Global Aviation, ExxonMobil

"Sanyin's book is brilliant in its inspiration, instruction, and brevity. It is certain to build confidence and increase the odds of success for any person or organization attempting a change process."

David Kohler, President and CEO, Kohler Co.

"For those suffering from the malaise of failure to launch, Sanyin has created the recipe for anyone who is looking to make that big change in their life. Her methodical approach to making big changes digestible is the formula that get people off the sidelines and in the game."
Devin Johnson, President & COO, Uninterrupted, a Sports Digital Media company founded by LeBron James and Maverick Carter

"Sanyin Siang gets our attention and gets us organized and confident to take the big step."
Linda Klein, President, American Bar Association

"Sanyin Siang is a brilliant leader and catalyst who brings out the best in others. In this stimulating, insightful book she helps us all envision new launches—wherever we are in our vocations. Exciting to read – and even more important to implement!"
L. Gregory Jones, Provost, Baylor University

"*The Launch Book*, like it's author, is thoughtful and honest – it so genuinely wants its readers to succeed. The aggregated guidance and stories from real industry winners makes it that much more authentic and helpful, regardless of your stage of launching."
Julia Collins, Co-founder, GirlStarter

"Sanyin Siang has written a must-read for anyone ready for personal change. Her book provides readers with the tools, inspiration and motivation to become better, stronger, more authentic – even happier – versions of themselves."
Paul S. Amos II, President, Aflac

"I'm always looking for new ways to stimulate personal growth and Sanyin Siang's *The Launch Book* is just the ticket! She weaves together keen observations from her work and a terrific personal story, all to help us become better versions of ourselves. Well done!"
F. William McNabb, Chairman and CEO, Vanguard

"Sanyin has brought boundless passion, generosity and insight to launches of all kinds and is at the centre of an impressive tribe of business-builders. In *The Launch Book*, Sanyin teaches a leadership mindset that works: starting with self-awareness and finding a shared sense of purpose to power the launch through the inevitable obstacles and willpower depletion."
Dan Singer, Partner and Head of McKinsey & Company Global Sports & Gaming Practice

"For anyone looking to become a better version of themselves, *The Launch Book* is for you! It helps its readers be braver, more resilient, and more authentic in pursuing not only their next move, but also the right move. Empathic and encouraging, Sanyin also writes with honesty and vulnerability about how she puts the concepts from the book into practice in launching *The Launch Book*."
Angela Ruggiero, Olympic Champion, IOC Board Member, and Co-Founder, Sports Innovation Lab

"Sanyin Siang is one of the most inspiring leadership thinkers in America today. She cares deeply about helping what every motivated person so deeply desires – to achieve the breakthroughs necessary to realize their potential and live a life of truth and purpose. In her gorgeous new book, *The Launch Book*, Sanyin shows how we can all overcome the real barriers and discover what is genuinely possible."
James M. Citrin, Leader, Spencer Stuart CEO Practice and Author of *The Career Playbook*

THE LAUNCH BOOK

MOTIVATIONAL STORIES TO LAUNCH YOUR IDEA, BUSINESS OR NEXT CAREER

SANYIN SIANG

Published by
LID Publishing Ltd
One Adam Street
London
WC2N 6LE
United Kingdom

31 West 34th Street, Suite 8004,
New York, NY 10001, US

info@lidpublishing.com
www.lidpublishing.com

A member of:

BPR
Business Publishers Roundtable

www.businesspublishersroundtable.com

© Sanyin Siang, 2017
© LID Publishing Ltd, 2017

Printed in the Czech Republic by Finidr

ISBN: 978-1-910649-98-5

Cover and page design: Caroline Li
Illustrations: Sara Taheri

THE
LAUNCH
BOOK

MOTIVATIONAL STORIES TO LAUNCH
YOUR IDEA, BUSINESS OR NEXT CAREER

SANYIN SIANG

LONDON   NEW YORK   BOGOTA
MADRID   BARCELONA   BUENOS AIRES
MEXICO CITY   MONTERREY   SAN FRANCISCO
SHANGHAI

FOR OTHER TITLES
IN THE SERIES...

CONCISE
ADVICE
LAB

SMALL BOOKS: BIG IDEAS

CLEVER CONTENT, DYNAMIC IDEAS, PRACTICAL
SOLUTIONS AND ENGAGING VISUALS –
A CATALYST TO INSPIRE NEW WAYS OF THINKING
AND PROBLEM-SOLVING IN A COMPLEX WORLD

conciseadvicelab.com

CONTENTS

THE FUNDAMENTALS OF LAUNCH   xii

INTRODUCTION   xvi

PART 1   **BE: START WITH YOU**   xx

CHAPTER 1   IN THE BEGINNING   2
CHAPTER 2   BEING YOU   5
CHAPTER 3   CONTROLLING TIME   10
CHAPTER 4   FIND YOUR WHY   15
CHAPTER 5   ORIGIN STORY   20
CHAPTER 6   BE BRAVE   27
CHAPTER 7   BE VULNERABLE   30

PART 2   **ENGAGE: BUILD YOUR TRIBE**   34

CHAPTER 8   FIND YOUR MENTORS   36
CHAPTER 9   EMBRACE DIFFERENT   42
CHAPTER 10   LOVE THE TRUTH TELLERS AND NAYSAYERS   45
CHAPTER 11   CO-CREATE WITH YOUR CUSTOMERS   50
CHAPTER 12   GOOD IDEAS CAN COME FROM ANYWHERE   57

PART 3	**IMAGINE: DISCOVER THE POSSIBLE**	60
CHAPTER 13	PLAN FOR LUCK	62
CHAPTER 14	FIND YOUR FUN	67
CHAPTER 15	GOING FOR IT	74
CHAPTER 16	BRILLIANT FAILURES	80
CHAPTER 17	QUESTIONS IN SEARCH OF ANSWERS	85
PART 4	**NEXT PLAY**	92
CHAPTER 18	PIVOTS AND REFRAME	94
CHAPTER 19	TIMING	100
CHAPTER 20	BELIEF	103
CHAPTER 21	BE YOUR BEST YOU	109
PART 5	**LAUNCHING THE LAUNCH BOOK**	114
THE INSIDE LOOK		116
ACKNOWLEDGEMENT		131
ABOUT THE AUTHOR		132

THE FUNDAMENTALS OF LAUNCH

What is a launch? Whether it's about starting a new habit or a new business, what is inherent in every launch is change. It's change from the progression of the current path into a newly imagined one. It's change from the status quo. That's why launches can be energetic – and also why they can be so hard to initiate.

There's the fear of failure. What if you don't manage to achieve the outcomes you first imagined when the idea for the launch first surfaced? That thought alone can keep you from ever taking the first step.

Wouldn't it be better to work on all of the tactics surrounding the launch? For example, in thinking about a new career, it's easy to jump into tactics such as the wording of a résumé or, for a new project, to start working out the action plan – simply because those aspects are tangible and feel controllable. While tempting, this would like be putting the cart in front of the horse.

A key mindset is to approach any launch process as a discovery process. The outcome is not always controllable. But you can control the inputs. And what you learn in the process can be the foundation for a future launch. It's a perspective that redefines success to be multi-factorial and beyond a measurable outcome. I once asked Jeff Weiner, CEO of LinkedIn, how he defined success. His answer? The day after LinkedIn's IPO, he came into the office and nothing had changed.

With this learning mindset, there are several fundamentals:

BE YOU

Why do we launch? We do so in order to be become a better version of our current self. We launch in pursuit of our best selves. Because of this, at the core of every launch is the question: 'Is this you?' Unless the launch is aligned with who you are and what you value, you will not have sufficient belief to sustain you through the downs. Nor will the ups be as fulfilling as you think. So, knowing who you are and who you are not is critical throughout the launch process. Be aware of how you react to the different parts of the journey and ask yourself why. Being aligned with the essence of you and with your distinctive strengths or superpowers will also make it easier to arrive at the compelling why for the launch, craft your origin story, and ensure that you remain energized throughout the process

BUILD YOUR TRIBE

No successful launch is ever done in a silo. Everyone needs emotional support, advice, feedback, championship, thought-partnership, and the ability to shape ideas for improvement and relevance. Not all of these can be found in one person. They need to be built with a tribe of people you can trust. This include mentors, truth-tellers and naysayers, cheerleaders and also customers. And in building a tribe for your launch, you are allowing others to invest in your success.

We all yearn to be part of something greater than ourselves that allows us to bring our talents to bear towards something worthwhile and sustainable. If your launch purpose is authentically you and meaningful, you can give others a space to belong through building a launch tribe.

As Kristen Titus, Chief Innovation Officer for New York, once told me, *"With any launch, to seed the ground with people who feel invested in your success, I launch with a braintrust. Behind you, behind the mission, and the powers that be, it's never about you, it's more than you."*

IMAGINE

If a launch is a change, unfettered by pre-existing notions of what is possible, then imagination is required. It's a constant dynamic of moving forward and shaping at the same time. You will go through many launches in a single lifetime, and you will also have smaller launches within a larger launch. The reality is, opportunities abound. You just need to be prepared for luck and go for it. And also know that thing which you will launch in five years, may not yet be imaginable.

If someone had told my twenty-something-year-old self that today I'd be able to create positive impact as the head of a leadership think-tank centre at a distinguished university and its business school, as a member of boards, an executive advisor and coach, writing a book, and being a mom to three wonderful children and wife to a remarkable man, I would have thought it all a stretch from the realms of possibility.

NEXT PLAY

Because you are always in movement, there's never sure footing on the steps, except knowing with each tread that you are in pursuit of becoming the best you. It's about being present while also being aware that there is a next play. Don't hold on to your ideas too dearly – you should hold them lightly so you can be more flexible and adaptable to maintain relevance and alignment with you.

GENEROSITY

What will enable you to have a more meaningful experience, regardless of the outcome, is a spirit of generosity. This attitude will also build up your resilience. Just as those in your tribe have invested in your success, by sharing and opening up to you their social, reputational, intellectual and financial capital, pay it forward by sharing these with others. As Ralph Waldo Emerson wrote, "Be ye an opener of doors for others." In doing so, in the end you may discover that you have invested in your own success in the long run.

INTRODUCTION

Throughout my leadership engagements with chief executives, entrepreneurs and students, I've encountered myriad questions and challenges. These questions often deal with pivoting to a new career path, introducing a new idea, or starting a new project or start-up. As varied in context as all of these may seem, I have found one common thread in what all of these professionals are looking for, the simple question: How do I launch?

While there are many books out there about the specifics of résumés, or communicating an idea, or the nuts and bolts of birthing a start-up, this book addresses a key factor that is often overlooked. To enable a successful and sustainable launch requires the right mindset.

What do I mean by this?

In an ideal world, the launch process would look like this:

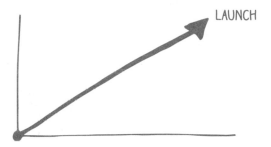

However, in reality, most ideas are like this:

or this:

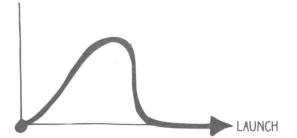

This isn't always a bad outcome because, on further exploration, there are ideas that should not be launched. However, for those ideas that can make an impact, a successful launch process is necessary and looks more like this.

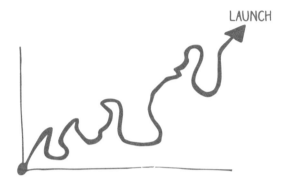

It's messy. It takes energy. There are psychological lifts and plunges. And at times it can be terrifying. I know. I empathize. I've been there.

This is my first book. Despite having written dozens of thought pieces that have appeared in *The Wall Street Journal*, *Fortune*, *Forbes*, *The Huffington Post* and *LinkedIn*, getting started on the process of writing a book is new, different and uncomfortable for me. The existence of this book proves the viability of its concepts.

But here's what I know from my journey, which includes drawing from those who have launched across so many different domains. It can also be beautiful, meaningful, AWESOME. And it can also be FUN.

Developing the right mindset can provide you with the psychological armour to battle the vacillations, the perspectives and the know-how in refining the ideation so that you can have the best chances to arrive at launch.

I can't promise that the outcome of reading this book will lead you to a successful launch. But I can promise that the concepts, stories and questions in this book will enable you to be more reflective and position you more ably for a positive experience and outcome. That outcome may actually be the decision not to launch because you are exactly where you should be. This book will help you to re-imagine and discover more about yourself. It will also help you to build strong relationships with others who join you on this journey.

And I don't want to provide you with only my thoughts and experiences. Throughout my career, I've had access to stories that have not yet been told and I will be sharing them with you here. Let's launch this journey together.

"We don't stop playing because we grow old;
we grow old because we stop playing."
– George Bernard Shaw

PART ONE

BE: START WITH YOU

CHAPTER 1
IN THE
BEGINNING

One morning, my seven-year-old daughter bounced into the bedroom.

"What do you want to order for breakfast, mom?" She handed me a multi-page menu, colourfully decorated and filled with squiggly lines with a sidebar outlining several drink options.

"I'd like some apple cider and an order of squiggly lines, please."

She left and returned with several cut-outs. She had drawn and coloured glasses, a slice of brown bacon, a jug of cider, a white plate. So, at some point that morning, she had had the idea to do this. And then, something inspired her to move forward with the idea. Next, she took time to think about the output and expanded the energy to draw and diligently create a multiple-page menu and cut out each little part of the order. What sparked all of this?

I asked what made her move forward with the idea. Her response?

"Well, Daddy was asking me whether I wanted cereal or yoghurt for breakfast. I told him I wanted a sandwich. And he said, 'No. What

do you think this is? A restaurant?' And I said, 'Yes!' That's how I got the idea of making a menu because my restaurant needs a menu.

I thought it would be a fun activity for me. I love art. And I knew you would love it, mom. I could put a lot of effort into it and it would be one of my creative things."

This story illustrates two things:

First, that ideation and inspiration are happening all the time. In a given day, all of us are making decisions to launch something, trivial or major. The scale may differ, but the notions around motivation and expansion of energy, and the risks of engaging in the process are the same.

Second, the notion that launching is a natural part of us. As children, we are unbounded by fear of failure and fear of rejection. Inspired by ideas and possibilities, we engage readily in the launch process and in doing so, discover more about who we are, our likes and dislikes, and have a ball doing so. But somewhere between then and adulthood, we grow more cautious. And with other demands on our attention and time, we also grow less motivated and less fun oriented.

If you can reframe the launch process as an opportunity to connect to the core of your creative self, you will have more fun. You will also see it as part of a journey of continuous discovery.

So, how can you enter into any launch journey?

First, you have to ask yourself two questions:

1. Who am I and who am I not? This question addresses what you value the most.

2. What is the compelling reason for this launch? The answer to this question will keep you going when you run into obstacles and help you find ways to punch forward to surf the waves of momentum.

CHAPTER 2
BEING YOU

> *"Be yourself. Everyone else is already taken."*
> – Oscar Wilde

In any launch you will face many obstacles, but your sense of belief is what will sustain you through the challenges. To truly believe in something, it has to have integrity with your values and who you are.

You may know Steve Wozniak as the co-founder of Apple. But Apple, as we know it, almost didn't happen. The first time a major investor offered him and Steve Jobs funding to start Apple, he turned it down.

Woz shares:

"I had a very good feeling of who I was and my core values from early in life. I knew that I wanted to be an engineer. I decided early in life that I wanted to be an engineer first, and a fifth-grade teacher second.

Apple had two starts. The first was Apple I, which told everyone in the world here is the formula for a personal computer. The second is Apple II and that's where we were going to start a company. We knew this was big money, but I wasn't interested after that. At that time, I'd developed two computers and a computer language in one year while moonlighting from HP. For me, HP was my job, as an engineer for life, and Apple was a side project. Our investor wouldn't go for that.

At first I turned down the opportunity because I had my goal to be an engineer at HP for life. Finally, a friend convinced me that I could start this company and remain an engineer. That day, I called Steve Jobs and said, OK, we are starting Apple."

What makes a launch stressful is the constant tug of discovering and making choices. To simplify things, the key heuristic in exploring a launch is whether it's right for you. It has to be aligned with who you are at the core. Woz just had it figured out earlier than most. He was an engineer who wanted to bring the things he imagined to life. And once they were able to position what he would be doing at Apple, it became an easy choice. Later on, after he retired from Apple, he was true to what he wanted to be. He became a fifth-grade teacher for many years.

So, with that in mind, how will you launch in line with your truest self? One way is to look at whether the environment is conducive and nurturing to that expression of who you are.

Carla Harris is a Wall Street powerhouse; she is the vice chairman and managing director at Morgan Stanley. What I admire about Carla is her wide range of talents – from being a gifted banker, noted speaker and author, to being an amazing gospel singer. I love the incredible way she can energize others in a room by giving them the space to bring their full selves to the table.

She is also very much herself.

"You can't suppress all the unique things that make you, because that is your competitive advantage. Being you is something you do best; better than anyone else, as much as they might try."

Core to her being is this driving force to make a positive impact in other people's lives. The reason she became a banker is because she saw the multiplier effect that bankers have. To her, if a company goes public and becomes successful, it can hire people and have a ripple effect in providing opportunities for so many others. Carla has never deviated from who she is at the core. And her advice is to find environments that continue to nurture that.[1]

"Part of being authentic is choosing a working environment or a job that lets you be you. It may not be the natural part of you, but you need to pick a seat where you can bring all of who you are to the table.

"I can come into Morgan Stanley one day as 'Carla the singer', and when it's time to be social, I become 'Carla the party person', and same for 'Carla the spiritual warrior' when necessary. When there is a deal that is not going well, I will skip lunch and tell my team that I am going to Mass to pray about it. I think you enhance yourself in any environment by bringing all of yourself to the table."

1 Comments excerpted from interview originally published at COLE LifeChats Collection

A big part is to understand what's important to you and how the platform, whether that's your career or business, is consistent with that.

One way of discovering who you are is to be attuned to what others are saying consistently about you.

Strategies for understanding who you are include:

- Be attuned to what energizes you.

- Keep track of what you spend a lot of your time doing; what are your default behaviours?

- Engage those around you. Ask them for behavioural feedback. If positive, unearth the aspects of your behaviour that lead to the good outcomes. If negative, dive into what can be improved.

- Do you have a mission statement for yourself? For example, here's mine – *My mission is not to be great, but to enable greatness.* That shapes how I advise, write, coach and engage with those around me.

BEHAVIOURAL ECONOMICS CONCEPT - WILLPOWER DEPLETION

When Mark Zuckerberg returned from paternity leave after the birth of his first child, he posted a picture on Facebook of his closet with the question, "What should I wear?" The picture shows a rack of identical grey t-shirts hung neatly, making the choice of not making a choice whimsical. What seemed like a funny picture is actually a brilliant strategy on Zuckerberg's part to prevent willpower depletion in his life.

Research shows that the more choices you make, the less you are able to make sound choices. So, by eliminating a choice, he was reserving his willpower for later. This is the reason why making important decisions earlier in the day has a better chance of a positive outcome than making them at the end of the day.

What this means is that if you are making a lot of decisions, you will have to deal with depletion. Even if you are able to make a lot of decisions, you will be exhausted from making them because you have to think so much every single time. So even if you are able to overcome choice overload, it can still be exhausting.

The easiest way to reduce the cognitive, and sometimes monetary and time effort that choices take, is to come up with a decision heuristic. The decision heuristic you should have is, 'Is this me?' Make that your equivalent of a closet full of grey t-shirts. Save your willpower and energy for other decisions.

CHAPTER 3
CONTROLLING
TIME

*"The day is of infinite length for him who knows
how to appreciate and use it."*
– Johanne Wolfgang von Goethe

Time is one of the biggest constraints in a launch. Yet we often underestimate the time required for a task, or feel overwhelmed because of the seeming lack of time. A successful launch process requires us to get a handle on how we relate to time and be disciplined in how we use it.

This summer, I was part of the 86th Joint Civilian Orientation Task Force, where 35 civilians were guests of the US Secretary of Defense, and we were granted unprecedented access to all five branches of military service. One of the visits was to US Army Special Operations Command, home to the Green Berets, Rangers and other members of the army's special forces.

We learned a startling fact. The margin of time error for any mission? Thirty seconds. When you think about the number of things that could go wrong every step of the way – from a Blackhawk needing to be repaired right before take off, to weather conditions, to unfathomable uncertainties – the complexities of the mission within that margin of error and the exquisiteness of planning is mind boggling.

During the visit, we spent some time with Lt. Gen. Ken Tovo, Commander of US Army Special Operations. When we asked him what one thing he would most like to have right now, his answer surprised us.

Time.

Time for his troops to come back and get re-energized before being deployed again. Time for them to spend with their families. Time in a day to wrestle with the minutia of a major command and time to think. Time is a multiplier effect for positive impact.

If I were to stage a revolt against the tyranny of time today, there would be many followers. The consistent thing I hear is the fleetingness of time. And the compression of time in today's frenzied existence. Our ability to control time is what we all crave most.

Lisa Shalett felt the full force of time and perception when she launched a new chapter in her career. Lisa had been at Goldman Sachs for 20 years. As a partner, she had headed up three key divisions during her tenure: Global Brand Marketing & Digital Strategy, International Equities Sales & Trading, and Compliance, Legal & Audit.

She is also one of the most intentional and self-aware people I've ever met. An East Asian Literature Studies major, who asks the most soul-illuminating questions – did I mention that she doesn't fit your typical image of an ace investment banker? When her children were in high school, she made a decision to spend more time with them before they headed off to college; she retired from Goldman and the career she had known for two decades.

Driven by her values, her launch was into new possibilities, platforms and a new relationship with time. She shares:

"Going from 200 mph to suddenly having to figure out what to do with your time – for the first time in a long time, having control over your time, and having unstructured time. You realize that no one taught you how to do that. You've always been BUSY and PRODUCTIVE and on the go. Time has been a constraint – there is never enough of it – and, as such, being idle has never been an option.

"Constraints make us creative. So, it is kind of scary when those constraints are removed. You have to change the metrics you use to assess yourself, change many ways in which you have been wired. You also have to change your relationship with time – how you think about it; surprisingly, rather than feel time as an abundance, you will feel even more the preciousness of it and the importance of allocating it thoughtfully."

So while Tovo felt the compression of time, Lisa, when faced with it in abundance, recognized the way to control it is to be intentional with its usage. This is no different with corporate launch projects as well. And part of the challenge is dealing with potential distractions. Being intentional requires knowing what to focus on.

Luckily, time is not a constant. How you relate to it is based on your perception as much as it is on the precision of each nanosecond. Behavioural economists use this concept to enhance the experience of waiting in line and queues at amusement parks and entertainment venues. At Disney, the snaking line creates the perception of a shorter wait. Having different distractions along the queue also creates a faster passage for a seemingly mundane task.

You can use your perception of time to play to your advantages. If you are going to launch properly, you need to be able to stretch and compress time.

It doesn't have to be long. A way to stretch time is to step outside from your normal frame of reference and give your brain a rest from the task at hand.

How can you control time to stretch it and use it intentionally to create possibilities? Here are five ideas that wouldn't take up much time:

1. Schedule 5 minutes a day to do nothing. Make it deliberate and at the same time each day.
2. Spend 5 minutes each day to connect with a friend. It can be sending them a text, an email, a Facebook message.
3. Schedule 5 minutes each day to write a positive note. Many leaders, from Pat Miller (co-founder of Vera Bradley) to Shelly Lazarus (Chair Emeritus Ogilvy & Mather and GE Board Director), write handwritten well-done notes to their employees.
4. Schedule 5 minutes a day to read something different from your everyday work. It can be a page from the dictionary, a comic strip or an article.
5. Set aside an hour of solitude for working on your launch process.

Each of these ideas can create reference points. Bill Wright-Swadel is one of the foremost millennial career experts in the US. What I admire about Bill is that no matter how administrative his role becomes, he carves out a significant portion of his time to engage and mentor students. He is also deeply philosophical. One day, he shared this profound quote on time with me:

"Life at its most meaningful is often circular. Yet, when it spins, it loses the purposeful passing of a consistent point of reference. The comfort and learning implicit in repetition becomes a blurred set of images – seen too often. Slowed by the visionary who quits the spiral, the circle of life returns its gifts in full measure."

I think of walking in a forest and creating markers so we don't become lost. So we can be reminded that we've been here before. That's the role of reflection and scheduling in time away. Bill's words made me think of reference points and why we sometimes need to step out of our frame of reference in order to gain clarity on what these reference points are.

CHAPTER 4
FIND YOUR
WHY

*"The two most important days in your life are the day
you were born, and the day you find out why."*
– Mark Twain

There's nothing wrong with chasing perfection, universal adulation or fame and fortune. For many, these chases can be some of the most compelling motivators to launch. However, if they are the only goals for the launch, they aren't going to be enough to sustain you through the ups and downs of the journey.

First, these outcomes are unpredictable and not fully within your control. And then, even if you were able to reach them, you may discover a brief jolt of elation – but they won't be entirely fulfilling. Such is the way of vanity chases.

The secret for the most successful launchers I know is that they have found the 'why', the compelling factor of their launch journeys. And that why is something meaningful. The end goal ceases to be an end-all, but rather a means to a greater end. They may not have always known what that why was at the beginning of the launch process, but they discover it somewhere along the journey.

Bob McDonald, 12th Chairman, President & Chief Executive Officer of The Procter & Gamble Company, once shared what has fuelled his rise to the top of his profession in his careers. His answer is that he never aspired to be the CEO.[2]

"Early on in my life, in my career, I decided the measure of success is how many people I can help. Your ambition has to be for the organization, not yourself. If the ambition is for yourself, you're not going to achieve anything; no one will follow you because you will be an inauthentic leader. So I think the best thing to do is decide what your personal satisfaction is, define your own success, factors and follow your purpose to achieve that end rather than allowing external factors to define that end for you."

At this point, you may think – great, but this all sounds awfully idealistic and abstract. How do you unearth that meaning? And does it really help?

The best way to explain this is through the following story:

If you ever meet Scott Pioli, you'll see a towering man with a humble attitude that hides how badass he is in his profession. If you are a fan of the New England Patriots, the Kansas City Chiefs or the Atlanta Falcons, you'll most likely want to pepper him with questions about draft picks, game plays and his three Super Bowl victories. But, you wouldn't expect him to be one of the fiercest champions for diversity and inclusion in the NFL.

2 Excerpted from interview originally published in *Forbes* and LinkedIn. https://www.linkedin.com/pulse/us-veterans-affairs-secretary-dont-ask-me-how-become-ceo-sanyin-siang

Besides the fact that his efforts are an important cause, and good for the sports industry, I wondered what drives him?

It is to do with his background. Scott grew up in Washingtonville, New York, a town of blue-collar workers, many of whom did not go to college. His athletic prowess earned him a football scholarship to Central Connecticut State College University, which opened up doors and changed the trajectory of his life.

Scott was the first from his family to graduate from college. But that shouldn't have been the case. Scott had two older sisters who were more gifted athletes and, as Scott acknowledges, better students, both of whom would have also received college scholarships today. Back then, Title IX existed but was mostly ignored throughout the country. And instead, they both stayed in his home town.

He explains:

"The relationship capital that I have accumulated over these years and the three Super Bowl rings – all have a greater purpose. This is the most important part of it. To use the platform for change so that others might have the chance that I had, so that there's an equal playing field."

Thinking about his sisters, and being attuned to seeing the prevalence of race and gender inequality throughout his life and as he rose in the sports industry, led Scott to look at all of his different launches as building platforms that can enable him to help in the fight for diversity and inclusion. They became the driving force, the meaning behind his 'why'.

Tracie Rotter, a partner at GV (Google Ventures), has seen launches and the meaningful why behind a launch take on different forms.

"Let's say you take your first job out of college and as you grow and develop your individual sense of self and understand the areas where you want to contribute to the world, you discover those things may not align with where you are."

Sometimes a launch happens instead of going through a deliberate process. What happens to the meaningful why then?

A couple years ago, my friend Andrea Bridges looked around her 900 square foot, two bedroom, one bath home and thought of her two kids and another along the way. The family decided not to move because they loved the neighbourhood. But, they also needed more space, which meant a renovation and an addition. Andrea imagined living in the throes of sawdust, noise and mess. It was already overwhelming. But that was the only option. Sometimes, the only option to reach one's aspiration is a launch.

What Andrea discovered was dealing with construction and the tangible effects was the easy part. The hard part was the decisions that went into every detail – from how the kitchen should be reconfigured, to which tiles to use in the bathroom, to where to place the laundry.

We tend to think about renovation or construction as either tied to function or beauty, a home is an intimate space. While this was all within the constraints of an existing footprint, Andrea discovered each decision was tied to something deeper. For example, the resulting kitchen had a large island with a butcher block countertop for her family's ritual of pie-making, and it opened to the dining room and porch to allow for entertaining many guests. The renovation process, the launch, was not only an expression of their personal aesthetics, but an expression of who her family is, how they interact with each other, and how they engage with guests who come through the doors.

The launch process became a discovery process – a discovery of how her family lived, interacted and engaged with their friends and community This process was an opportunity for every member of her family to give voice and contribute to a shared family project. It was about being present with one another, which became the meaningful why behind the launch of her renovation project.

If every launch is an expression of who you are, your values and beliefs, finding the meaningful 'why' not only gives you and others clarity for the launch, but also gives you goals worth pursuing.

CHAPTER 5
ORIGIN STORY

"The world is not made of atoms. It is made of stories."
— Muriel Rukeyser

Every superhero has an origin story. So if you think about you or your idea as the hero of your launch, wouldn't it make sense for you to have an origin story too?

Super hip behavioural economist, Troy Campbell, sums up the purpose of an origin story best:

"Behind that idea of an origin story is not that a moment changed me. It's that a moment revealed me."

What then makes for a good origin story? In *Spiderman*, is it the moment he gets bitten by the radioactive spider, transforming his physical powers, as well as his destiny? Or is it another part of his journey?

The heart of the origin story reveals your motivation, your 'why'. In *Spiderman*, the origin story isn't about being bitten by a spider

– that doesn't reveal who he is or how his character is formed. Spiderman's origin story begins when his uncle Ben is shot – Spiderman could have stopped the villain but he didn't. This results in personal tragedy and him realizing that "with great power comes great responsibility". And, therefore, his entire conflict is about protecting the people he loves and fighting crime to prevent other tragedies.

Compelling origin stories not only reveal the motivation but also create a level of authentication and connection.

A few years ago, I was invited by the Krzyzewski family to join the Emily K Center Board of Directors. It was a great honour, but if I was going to sign on, I wanted to be an ace contributor. To do that, I needed to passionately believe in it.

The centre tackled education, an issue that I felt strongly about. It focused on Durham, which was my home community. It had a record of tremendous success in terms of impact, and its founder, Coach Mike Krzyzewski, is a leader who I love and admire and whose values undergird the centre that I run.

But what drove my decision to join is the origin story of the centre. Coach K is a first-generation college graduate. He tells the story of sitting at the kitchen table when his family received the acceptance letter to the United States Military Academy. That moment changed the trajectory of his life. For his future generations, college would now be a norm and not an exception.

And it was because his mother, Emily Krzyzewski, believed in him.

So when Coach was at a point in his life when he had the means and platform to help transform the lives of kids who were like him, he founded the centre in honour of the woman who had launched him on his path.

When I learned that the centre focused on first-generation college hopefuls in the education space and in its flagship programme, and took them from early childhood to college, I got excited. I am not a first-generation college graduate, but I am a first-generation immigrant. I know what it's like to never be a full part of your former community and never quite be a member of your new community.

When you are a first generation anything, you are in between worlds. You have to be brave and you have to dream. Those kids that the Emily K Center is trying to help – I get them. Those kids were me.

Coach shares: *"Each kid has their own story ... Their goals and dreams become our hopes and dreams."*

The origin story of the Emily K Center is powerful and authentic. Hearing it enabled me not only to believe in it deeply, but also to relate to those it aims to serve. Serving on this centre's board is one of the most meaningful things I've ever done.

Why is an origin story important? It's what makes you, well you. Imagine you are an investor or a hiring manager or that person whose buy-in is key to someone's launch journey. Now imagine you are looking at other start-ups, other candidates, other opportunities.

What's going to compel you to help them? Is it their skills or knowledge? Those who lack it can remedy it with time and mentorship. Or is it something more magical? That defies imitation? It's the genuine passion and motivation. If understanding the genesis of your motivation and passion is a key part of the process, then to make you and others feel that 'why', you need to frame that into a story.

Stories are information put into a context that's emotionally resonant. As a faculty member of Duke's Story Lab to explore different forms of storytelling, I've seen how our brains are wired to receive stories more readily than straight data.

Stories create powerful emotions. When you experience an idea or information through a narrative, you actually experience biological changes in your body. Your brain produces higher levels of a chemical called oxytocin, which is associated with empathy, feelings of closeness, affinity and kinship. Biologically, you can feel closer to the person who you are entering a story with.

Not only that, stories can transport you to another world. There is a phrase for this – narrative transportation. In the process, it moves you to an action.

The first time I saw Caryl Stern on the stage to make a case for UNICEF, she started with a story. On the screen was a black and white picture of a little girl from the 1930s next to the picture of a ship.

"That little girl," she told us, "was sent away by her parents, out of Nazi Germany, to safety in America."

My heart felt a knot. That little girl in the picture was the same age as my child. I couldn't imagine having to say goodbye to my children.

Caryl continued, *"That girl survived and was adopted and cared for lovingly by her new family who gave her a new future."* She went on to explain that that little girl was her mother.

The other picture showed a picture of a ship that her dad was on. He was able to get a ticket on the ship to escape Germany. The ship reached the US, only to be turned back to Europe. On a brief stop in London, her dad was arrested and thrown in jail. That saved his life. Everyone else on the ship got sent back to Germany and perished in the Holocaust.

The two stories that Caryl told us about her personal history revealed a deeper understanding of why she was a passionate humanitarian and child advocate. Caryl is CEO of UNICEF USA. A gifted storyteller, she uses stories to illustrate her points.

Because of her moving narrative, coupled with the revelation of her origin story, we were all inspired to donate money. She is one of the most successful fundraisers, having raised more than $500 million to eradicate childhood diseases around the world.

Beyond driving you to action, origin stories also set up a destiny story, which in your case, is the result of your launch story.

I've personally leaned-in on origin stories for my own launches. I'll share the application of the origin story in another passion project of mine.

A few years ago, my then four-year-old daughter asked me to help her solve a problem.

"Go try and figure it out yourself," I told her.

"I can't," she answered.

"Why not?" I asked.

"Because I don't have a prince with a sword."

That was the problem. We started looking for books and media for girls aged 4-9 about princesses who solve problems. To our dismay, we couldn't find any. So we sat down and created *The Thinking Cap Princess* series. Rather than fight the princess identity, we were going to reclaim the princess as a problem-solver. And the princesses were going to work together in teams, use their IQ and EQ, and their strengths across different disciplines to tackle the toughest challenges.

Isn't that much more compelling than saying I'm creating a children's series about princesses who solve problems? When you are able to articulate the origin story for your launch, you can create a more authentic resonance.

ORIGIN STORY EXERCISE

Eileen Chow, co-founder of Duke's Story Lab, is one of the foremost story experts I know. This is a simple exercise she does with students in her Story World classes to unearth the origin story.

1. Describe yourself using three facts. Write those down.

    _____

2. Describe yourself again, this time, using a different set of three facts. Write those down.

    _____

3. Describe yourself again, using another set of three facts.

    _____

Then ask: What do you see? How do these facts connect to your launch story?

Why do you care about this launch? We won't care unless you show us that you care.

Through story form, you can articulate why you do what you do. In the process of doing that, you not only show others why you care, you can make them care.

CHAPTER 6
BE BRAVE

> *"You are braver than you believe,*
> *stronger than you seem,*
> *and smarter than you think."*
> – A. A. Milne in *Winnie the Pooh*

Every launch is a change from the status quo. And change is un-comfortable, ushering in a degree of uncertainty. So whether you are launching a new job, a new project or even a new habit, it requires a degree of gumption. You need to be brave.

So what holds up bravery? It can be a sense of purpose, a desire to do the right thing and having the courage to fail. It also requires a degree of vulnerability.

One of my best friends, Anne Shee (CC) Lee is a mom of four and a Harvard-trained paediatrician. She is the most tender-hearted person I know. She also spends several months of the year travelling to Bangladesh where there are high rates of infant death. CC is one of the world's foremost experts on newborn health.

When she was in her residency, she volunteered in the cities with children who did not have access to top medical care. That work compelled her to pursue a public health degree with Johns Hopkins University.

Early on, on one of her trips to Tibet, she got called to see an infant who was born healthy, but had suddenly stopped breathing. No one knew how to resuscitate it. By the time CC arrived, the baby was too far gone and died in her arms. That experience, and subsequent ones involving preventable infant deaths in rural areas, led her to launch a new NGO. Called 'Deliver', it's designed to train locals in places with low access to healthcare.

Another example, from a corporate domain, is Kerrii Anderson, a seasoned executive with board service experience in companies such as Chiquita, LabCorp and Worthington Steel.

When she was named the CEO of Wendy's, sales were still declining quarter after quarter. She had also inherited the Red Wig marketing campaign, where everyone in the ads wore red wigs. Created by a premier advertising firm, the campaign was memorable, but Kerrii felt it did not represent the brand: "We were about great food and service and not red wigs."

Though she was an accountant and not a marketing expert, she could feel the unrest in the franchise population. So, at the Wendy's National Advertising Association meeting, she and another firm presented a pitch for a campaign that would take them back to the Wendy's cameo.

"It was the most nervous moment of my life. And then I thought if I can't be brave and courageous now, I had to do what I think needs to be done. I say to everyone – trust your gut. When it's all said and done, I could go to sleep and I could say, it was the right thing to do. It was one of the most memorable, rewarding, ballsy things I ever did. In my heart of heart, it was the right thing to do. I knew it wasn't going to be easy. And I knew it better work!"

The franchisees agreed and the new campaign got things back on track. Sales began to increase. It changed the attitude and mindset of the franchisees who were embarrassed by what was running on TV.

All these changes require certain acts of courage. It's not revolutionary. You are pivoting around who you are and your values. The platforms are just different. It goes back to the values and principles.

CHAPTER 7
BE
VULNERABLE

"Vulnerability is the birthplace of innovation, creativity and change."
– Brené Brown

Bravery also requires a degree of vulnerability.

Marshall Goldsmith is among the world's foremost executive coaches. He has coached more than 150 CEOs, including those at Ford, Walmart, Best Buy, Intel, Pfizer, and authored *NY Times* best-sellers. I met Marshall when he launched a legacy project to mentor the next generation of top executive coaches for the world. Out of 12,000 applications, he selected an initial group of 25 mentees. As one of the 25, I heard this personal story from Marshall.

Marshall had hired someone whose job was to phone him every day and for five minutes, read through a set of questions that he had written up and listen to his answers.

He was asked:

Did you do your best to
- ■ be happy?
- ■ find meaning? Be fully engaged?
- ■ build positive relationships?
- ■ set clear goals?
- ■ make progress towards goal achievement?

Why did Marshall do this? He explained:

"Because it is too hard and we are all too cowardly to do this by ourselves."

So Marshall hired someone to keep him accountable.

An open confrontation with yourself is the key to behavioural change. It's not about planning to change; it's having the courage to launch change, to launch the process with minute steps, however small, and be disciplined in the seemingly mundane repetition of a thoughtful process.

When you are feeling vulnerable, which can often be the case when faced with uncertainties in the launch process, there is a tendency to put up a wall. And that wall is often in the form of projecting the answers we know. You should not be dismissive of your own vulnerability.

Ellen Kullman, is a retired CEO of Dupont and serves on the Board of Carbon 3D, Dell Computers and Goldman Sachs. Earlier in her career, she was asked to lead a new division when Dupont moved from the chemicals business into safety consulting. At that point, she had been in her role for three and a half years as VP of the business.

Ellen explains:

"Everybody said, 'No, you shouldn't do it.' I was comfortable. And that comfortableness made me uncomfortable, because I was getting to the part where I wanted to try something different."

When they started the business, it wasn't smooth going. They failed a lot. They would gather on Friday afternoons with a small team of people to dissect what worked, what didn't, and what needed to change. The meetings also encouraged team members to be open about the angst and uncertainty that they were feeling so they could tackle those feelings together.

"Everybody had a get-out-of-jail free card, nobody felt their career was going to be hurt by doing this, but there was a real sense of pride and a real sense of loyalty that kept us going and kept us surviving."

That vulnerability created a safe space for them to really tackle the problem and eventually led to the success of the new division.

The person that helps you when you face your own vulnerabilities may be yourself.

Research[3] shows that vulnerability can be powerful. In a study on underdog brands, researchers found that customers prefer brands that highlight a humble beginning or "a passion to triumph against the odds".

While on maternity leave several years ago, I made the mistake of catching up on reading women's fashion magazines. In one magazine, all the

3 https://hbr.org/2010/11/capitalizing-on-the-underdog-effect

women featured were perfect. The impression I got was that they were mothers with multiple well-behaved children, who had coiffed hair, effortlessly fashionable executives who also chaired multiple charities and lived in designer homes, where there wasn't a single thing out of place. And they also never had a bad day.

I looked in the mirror and saw dark circles under my eyes, hair that wouldn't stay in place, piles of papers everywhere around my house, and I was starting to have a bad day. Rather than inspiring me, these articles were creating a sense of anxiety. *"These types of lives are the norm,"* they seem to say. *"If you aren't like this, then you've failed."*

There I was, launching a new phase in my life – that of motherhood and, already, I was a failure.

Those articles and pictures were, as inspiring as they tried to be, accomplishing the opposite. What happened? They weren't relatable because there was no sense of vulnerability.

When I returned to Duke, we launched an Interview series – the COLE LifeChats. I started interviewing top women leaders. But, instead of asking them only about their best moments, I asked them to share a time of self-doubt, of facing failure. If they were to inspire the reader, the reader had to see their story and their challenges in these stories. And then, the answers and the subsequent success would be more helpful.

Sharing your vulnerabilities might inspire someone else. It might help a person who is facing the same challenges and help them get through their problems. In the process, you may earn another champion for your tribe. By being vulnerable, you enable others to invest in your success and help you be brave.

"No story is told alone"
– Duke University Story Lab motto

PART TWO

ENGAGE: BUILD YOUR TRIBE

CHAPTER 8
FIND YOUR
MENTORS

*"A mentor is someone who allows you
to see the hope inside yourself."*
– Oprah Winfrey

In the same way that it takes a village to raise a child, a successful launch requires a tribe. You may be a solo launcher but, if you are to have a chance at success, you can't approach it as a solo endeavour. Those you engage with on this journey are the members of your tribe. Tribes are different from networks because their existence in your life also provides a degree of emotional support. They can champion you fiercely, tell you the honest to goodness truth, connect you with key people, and keep you relevant. Mentors are one of the most important members of your 'launch tribe'.

Mentors can play different roles. I asked Meg Whitman,[1] CEO of Hewlett Packard Enterprise, about mentors who had made a significant impact in her life. She immediately responded with the names of two people.

1 Comments excerpted from interview originally published at COLE LifeChats Collection

One was Frank Wells, president and chief operating officer at Disney.

Meg told me:

"I would be in all of these high level meetings. He pulled me aside and said, 'Meg, you are just as smart as the guys. Speak up! Speak up!' I said, 'But, you know they sound like they've thought of everything ...' He went on, 'Trust me. They haven't. They're just talking. So, you should say what you think.' So, that's the kind of thing he did for me. And it was really very, very powerful."

Another one of her mentors was Pete Wilson, Governor of California. When Meg ran for Governor, he helped her to understand the political landscape – how it worked, who she ought to meet and how the whole process worked.

Meg's stories illustrate the different types of roles that mentors can play. The first gave her a jolt of confidence, while the second gave her an understanding of context.

I asked Jaunique Sealey, a serial entrepreneur who has spearheaded the launch of a luxury skincare company on QVC, the same question. In her case, her mentor, the rock icon Prince, helped her to get out of her comfort zone to rethink and expand her capabilities.

An engineer and lawyer by training, she had spent most of her career working on the business side of the music industry. She joined Prince's team, thinking her job would focus on legal contracts. Instead, one of her first projects was in tour management, to set up Prince's band for a televised performance. She had no prior knowledge of the complicated arrangement of instruments and equipment. A perfectionist, with an exacting attention to detail, being thrown feet-first into the high stakes of unknown projects was a recipe for failure.

And that day, the band didn't perform because they arrived to an empty set. Jaunique went home feeling defeated and expecting to be fired. Instead, Prince gave her a new assignment, this time not with the band, but with him directly.

This was part of Prince's methodology in creating a culture where his team members wouldn't be afraid to try new things. It was then that Jaunique realized that failure was not the end of the world.

Prince once shared a story about a close friend who had cultivated a spirit of freedom and fearlessness in the latter's young daughter. His friend would place her on the steps and tell her to jump and he'd catch her. He successively progressed her to higher and higher steps, but still, he'd catch her each time, even from the highest point. That spirit of fearlessness was what Prince wanted for his team. He wanted his team to not be afraid of spreading their wings beyond the familiar.

Prince became a valued and trusted mentor. He would often ask Jaunique: *"What do you want to do?"*

What Prince was trying to do was help her go beyond the perception of a defined role and dial into the core of what made Jaunique who she was – her passions and strongest talents. Because of Prince's mentorship, one of her guiding principles is to align her passions and talents with whatever endeavour she undertakes.

So what should you look for in a mentor? Lenny Mendonca, a retired Partner with McKinsey, who also founded *The McKinsey Quarterly* and mentors many entrepreneurs today, advises to look for those who have a genuine interest in your professional development – those who can be honest and give constructive feedback and who you can take along for the journey.

"A good mentor of mine described it to me as, 'If you want someone to enjoy your hobby, take them along with you, don't tell them to go get a hobby.' So, a participative mentor is much better than a talking mentor," Lenny shared.

Mentors help you feel like you matter, and that your voice and your ideas matter too.

If we all look into our personal histories, many of us will find our parents among our first mentors. My parents have given me the confidence to pursue my best self, always. My dad, a visionary, pushed me to reach for the impossible – just to see whether it was possible and showed me the fun of doing so. And from my mom, the pragmatist, I learned to look at failures as part of the learning process. Their mentorship taught me to always remember the generosity that others have given us and be quick to forget our generous acts to others. If their advice and ideas are seen throughout this book, well that's the upshot of how they've influenced my worldviews and interactions with others.

But while good mentors come to you serendipitously, how can you systematically become better at finding effective mentors? Here are some tips:

1. Don't look for mentors based on their position or title. This is one of the biggest mistakes I made early on in my career. I thought linearly. So, if I wanted to look at a role on paper, I tunnel visioned everything else out rather than see the fuller set of possibilities. However, throughout my career I have come to find that the best mentors I've had, have actually defied this logic. Today, some of them are my students. So, when looking for mentors, look at them as a whole person.

2. Have a diversity of mentors. Very few people can fulfil the full range of roles that mentors can play. Instead have multiple mentors – some call this a board of advisors. It's important to make sure they don't all look like you, or from the same industry with the same background. Diversity and plurality of mentors can give you a sense of the bigger picture and broaden your perspective; it will eliminate blind spots by challenging your existing point of view.

3. Be vulnerable. This matters. When I started mentoring, I discovered how less engaged I was when someone only showed their perfect side. It was hard to figure out where they needed help. I cheered for them, but I wasn't able to help them with challenges because they were never vulnerable enough to share the obstacles they faced. So be vulnerable and give your prospective mentors a chance to invest in your success.

4. Be a mentor yourself. How you get the most out of mentoring relationships is by being a mentor to others and being aware and attuned to how you are reacting throughout the interactions. Be a mentor to others and, by stepping into the shoes of mentorship, you become a more effective mentee.

5. Ask around. So how do you get a mentor? Sometimes all it takes is just engaging and asking questions.

6. Remember to follow up. Don't underestimate the value of follow ups. Loop back with them. Give them regular status updates on what's happening. Or how their advice has made you think, made you look at things differently or helped you along. When people take the time to speak with you – imagine a gazillion pulls on their time. Let them know that their investment in time has helped you. They mentor because they want to be helpful to your success. [Try out the template letter below]

MENTOR LETTER TEMPLATE

Dear:
Thank you for taking the time to speak with me and share your thoughts.

What was something they said – a feedback, or advice that stuck out?

As a result, what happened?

In the conversation, you mentioned interest in this. Can I be of help?
a. Make an introduction
b. Share an article that you come across
c. Provide a followup action

I look forward to keeping you updated on the progress of my launch.

CHAPTER 9
EMBRACE
DIFFERENT

"Talent perceives differences;
genius, unity."
– William Butler Yeats

When I worked at the American Association for the Advancement of Science (AAAS), the world's largest federation of scientific and engineering societies, my job was to explore the ethical, legal and social implications of technological advances such as cloning and cyberwarfare. It wasn't just about what was scientifically feasible, it was understanding how that science may change the way we think, interact, or even understand what it means to be human.

The job required talking and running across different networks and fields of expertise. Understanding the big picture ramifications and imagining what has not yet been imagined requires engaging scientists, policy makers, lawyers, media and the faith-based communities, who usually do not have the opportunity to engage in dialogue with each other. I discovered that specialization in different areas also meant stovepipes, unless you were intentional about jumping outside of your field to remove blinders and assumptions.

Often, the problem was like the story of the six blind men and the elephant. Each group would only be seeing their own parts were it not for the greater dialogue that enabled us to understand the effects of each part on the big picture.

If you draw upon more perspectives to understand the context, and the potential solutions, you'll have a higher probability of solving the right problem, and developing the most effective solution.

The best innovations are the result of collaboration. Edison, Einstein – they didn't work alone. Everyone knows the value of teamwork. And everyone knows that when you put together a team, it's important to work together to show each other's strengths. But, often when building teams, you tend to think more about function and staying inside a certain category.

People find it easier to cluster with those who are like-minded; organizations don't think enough outside the box about who their collaborators can be. How often do you think about going outside your comfort zone and common practices in terms of who you partner with or which organizations to partner with?

In an increasingly complex world, in which traditional boundaries are becoming less and less relevant, it may be unlikely for bedfellows to provide the most game changing and effective results.

To think out of the box, you have to connect out of the box. You have to embrace different.

For Baroness Martha Lane Fox, the key to success in her launches is building human capital and finding the best brains and diverse set of brains to think about problems. In 1998, Martha co-founded Lastminute.com, Europe's largest travel and leisure website, sold it and, from there, went on to launch doteveryone.org.uk. She is a crossbench peer in the UK House of Lords and also sits on the board of directors of Twitter. Launches are part of who she is.

She tells me:

"What I've enjoyed is unlocking problems and working out how to move things forward by listening to many different voices around the table. For example, our mission is to represent the world to everyone and not just the corporate world of the internet, to make the internet work for everyone, to make the UK fairer and better. In doing that, we've tried to bring together business leaders, charity leaders and people working in grassroots organizations in the UK."

What makes us different is our different lens of experiences, but what connects us is our humanity. We have to see each other's humanity first in order to celebrate the differences of the experiences that make the human whole.

Finally, to embrace different, you have to know you. Don't discount your unique self. What makes you different is also what makes you invaluable. And that means also understanding the type of role you might play in a launch.

To embrace different may also mean taking on different roles. You don't always have to be the one with the ideas. You may have the idea, but decide that you are not the one to launch, but someone else may be better and more effective and that's not the role you want to play.

CHAPTER 10
LOVE THE TRUTH
TELLERS AND
NAYSAYERS

"The dream begins with a teacher who believes in you,
who tugs and pushes and leads you to the next plateau,
sometimes poking you with a sharp stick called 'truth'."
- Dan Rather

If you are like me, you may tend to procrastinate on launches. Why?

An idea in the abstract can be as perfect as you imagine it. But, when starting the process and in clashing with reality, you encounter feedback – cringe-worthy feedback that may be counter to your imagined perfection. You may also encounter those who tell you 'no', who tell you that it's impossible and then proceed to list all the reasons why.

What can you do with these truth tellers and naysayers? While your gut might tell you to dismiss them or run away, you should embrace them instead. They can be among your most powerful allies for a successful launch.

First, truth tellers help to eliminate blind spots. Everyone's psychologically predisposed to having blind spots. Your experiences and beliefs inform you on how you see the world. Just like blinders placed on horses in busy city streets, blind spots can keep you focused, less reactive to distractions and help you make sense of the huge influx of data your brain receives each day. But a lack of awareness about your blind spots can keep you from vital information that opens up opportunities or prevents threats.[1]

There is a series of social psychology principles at work here.

People tend to overweigh information that confirms what they already believe, this results in 'confirmation' bias. If you have an entrenched belief, that belief can blind you to potential counterpoints. You now have access to so much information that you can always find something to confirm your beliefs. But what information are you not seeing?

'Availability' bias is a tendency to give greater credence to information that is commonly held by a greater number of people in a group, even when the information is all from a single source. Much has been made of the circulation of false news on social media sites. If people see a few shares of the same piece of news by those in their immediate circles, they are more predisposed to believing that news is true, regardless of its validity.

'Desensitization' bias is a tendency to project own experiences onto others when predicting their feelings; this can also create blind spots. When you encounter someone with an experience that you've never had, you tend to discount those experiences as less valid, or not true.

---

1 Excerpted from "Why We Fail to See What's In Plain Sight," by Sanyin Siang Forbes Nov 21, 2016.

And then there's 'attention gap' bias. This keeps your brain focused on one thing so you can complete a task but, in doing so, can prevent you from seeing other things that may be happening. Another term for this is 'tunnel vision'.

The confluence of the above natural biases prevents you from absorbing relevant data and validating new information. This keeps you complacently reliant on information from others in your social groups.

Just as physical blind spots can be dangerous, psychological blind spots can cause a failure of imagination with dire consequences in launches. They can keep you from seeing broader possibilities, or serious challenges to your dreams that you need to address.

To overcome blind spots, you need friends with gritty courage to tell you the truth. You need to be open to feedback and put your listening ears on.

First, it requires a mindset, a recognition that truth is a good thing. Jeff Jones, shared a story from one of the toughest times in his previous job. He had joined Target as Chief Marketing Officer. The company's culture was strong and it was also adored by customers. However, its traditions had created a fear of failure that became a major impediment to innovation and to quickly addressing crisis.

Then, crisis hit. Target encountered a credit card scandal that tested customers' trust and, overnight, its CEO resigned. In that moment of crisis, Jeff wrote to his employees (which he later published in a LinkedIn post titled, 'The Truth Hurts').[2]

2 "The Truth Hurts," by Jeff Jones, LinkedIn May 13, 2014

He writes:

"The reality is that our team members speaking with honesty is a gift. Because much of what they are saying is true. While we would have preferred to have a conversation like this with the team member directly, speaking openly and honestly, and challenging norms is exactly what we need to be doing today and every day going forward.

"Yes, the truth hurts. But it will also set you free.

"Our job now is to create a new truth and that is exactly what we are doing."

That crisis, and bold confrontation of truth and creating an open channel for which problems and issues could be discussed, led Target to survive crisis and launch into a more adaptive and innovative chapter.

How you create an environment that puts you in direct engagement with those who are your naysayers can enhance your chance of success. For example, Matthew Szulik, former CEO of Red Hat, is not an engineer by training. However, when he took the helm of a tech open source company, he needed to build credibility, trust and knowledge transfer with his engineering team. And there were many of the company's engineers who were not keen on him.

So, instead of the usual posh office associated with C-suite executives, he set up shop in a small office with no door, located right across from the free soda machine. By doing so, he created a natural pathway for engaging with every engineer, understanding the key issues the company faced, and creating a sense of shared ownership in the direction of the company.

In any launch process, it's critical to surround yourself with cheer-leaders and encouragers. But if you don't also engage the truth tellers and the naysayers, you may let your blindspots get the better of you and miss an opportunity at creating powerful advocates. And that's the truth.

CHAPTER 11
CO-CREATE
WITH YOUR
CUSTOMERS

"Part of co-creating with your customers is also being attuned to your distinctive strengths, your special point of view that no one else has because no one else has the same set of experiences that you do."
– Stephanie Mehta, Deputy Editor, Vanity Fair

In any launch, there is always a customer. In a home renovation, it's your family. In a career change, it's your potential employers and those in the industry. In a start-up, it's those whose problem you aim to solve. Because of this, no launch is ever done in a silo. Knowing who your customers are, and engaging them from the start, is key to any successful launch. Yet, this is a key group that most forget to engage.

However, you need to think beyond engagement. It's about asking them questions to understand the nature of the problem you are trying to solve with your launch. And then, listening to and incorporating their views and ideas. Essentially, you need to co-create with them. Why?

OFTEN, THEY MAY HAVE THE SOLUTION

In the magical James Thurber story, *Many Moons*, a princess is ill in bed for want of the moon. Her father, the king, calls in all his experts to figure out what the moon is and how to get it for her. They all fail. The jester asks the princess herself what the moon is. She answers that it's made of gold and the size of her fingernail. And with that, the problem is solved by gifting the princess with a little gold disc on a necklace.

Frances Hesselbein is one of the most acclaimed leaders in the world. A Presidential Medal of Freedom recipient and among *Time* magazine's '100 Most Influential People of 2016', she turned around the Girl Scouts of USA as CEO and co-developed the US Army's leader development model. A national treasure, she is also one of my dearest mentors.

A few years ago, she participated in New York City's 'Principal for a Day' programme, for top leaders throughout the city. Participants typically wanted the best and most prestigious schools. True to Frances, who looked at where she might be able to make the most difference, she asked for the city's worst school. They gave her a high school in the Bronx where there had not been a single graduate.

The first thing Frances did was ask the students what they needed. They asked for three things.

"Mrs. Hesselbein, could we have books for a library? And can some of those books be written by people who look like us?"

Frances raised funds for a library that included books by noted African American authors.

"Mrs. Hesselbein, can we have textbooks?"

Until then, the teachers had to photocopy pages from books for the students. Frances made a call to the Mayor's office and the textbooks arrived.

"Mrs. Hesselbein, can we have mentors in the business community?"

Frances got several businesses to sponsor the school and their employees became mentors for the students.

That year, there were 15 graduates from the school. Such is the power of asking those whom you are trying to serve, listening to their input, and using your powers to give them what they need. The solutions do not have to be complex. You might be surprised at how incredibly simple they are.

YOUR CUSTOMERS KNOW THE CONTEXT

There are general frameworks, but no one size fits all solutions. And just because you've been successful in one area, it doesn't necessarily mean you can apply the same model to the next iteration. Every launch has to be context-dependent and your customers are vital to the context.

Adam Klein is Chief Operating Officer of American Underground, a start-up hub based in North Carolina's Research Triangle. A key differentiator is that its home city of Durham has 100 plus years of start-up narrative from Black Wall Street, the financial hub for the African American community in the mid-20th century to today's foodpreneurs and tech start-ups. Because of this, Adam said:

"We can't build AU in the same image of Silicon Valley because we have different strengths and a different history."

They started with a failure – they had imagined a building with offices and co-working space for entrepreneurs. But no one showed up – for a year. Where they had gone wrong was in creating the space based on their prior successes in the office leasing industry. Then, Adam started talking to entrepreneurs about how they worked. Entrepreneurs like to cluster in teams and learn from each other. They also need fun to get their minds rejuvenated for problem solving.

Based on this, Adam and his team scrapped the layouts and furniture. They created brown bag lunch sessions for entrepreneurs to talk about lessons learned and bounce around ideas. And they converted the room that housed the old bank vault into a party room. In less than four years, AU has become one of the top start-up hubs in the country. Today, there are more than 350 start-ups under its umbrella. The group has outgrown its original space and has now expanded to two buildings.

Wendy Kopp, who started Teach for America (TFA) based on her college thesis, had been focused on helping each child reach their fullest potential through education in the US. But, she hadn't thought about expanding the organization globally. Then, in one year, she met 13 different people from different countries who asked about applying the TFA model to their countries.

This led to the launch of Teach for All. However, her team was smart to recognize that the issues may have local dependencies and so couldn't be done in exactly the same way as they were done in the US. So they engaged with the community to build a vision of shared outcomes and ownership.

"What we are putting in the centre of our work in any community is this effort to step back and step out of the constraints that we are in and with diverse actors starting with students and parents, respective community leaders, educators to ask – what do we want for our kids? This is a very different line of discussions. We believe it's important that those answers be very locally rooted with local values and aspirations and with the actual challenges facing the kids and the actual pathways to opportunity. Once we develop shared vision of student outcomes, we work backwards from there."

Because Wendy and her team recognized that there is not a 'one size fits all' solution, they co-created with their customers and stakeholders. Today, Teach for All is in 40 countries world-wide.

Many launches are made to build something that solves a problem that people have. Many launchers of ideas and projects start off with the following thought – I wish this existed. And they jump down that rabbit hole to explore it, if it's a problem that they want to solve in a space that they are passionate about.

But is that enough?

It's maybe important to solve your own problems, but you also need to validate and refine it as something that solves a problem that a larger group of people have.

I met Philip Winter, co-founder and CEO of Nebia, when I was a mentor for Praxis, a business accelerator focused on entrepreneurs with a larger purpose. Philip and his co-founder had produced a shower head that only required 30% water, without compromising the shower experience, to life. Their vision was to change the way the world consumes water.

When they launched on Kickstarter, they raised $3 million, got more than 400 international press mentions and Tim Cook, CEO of Apple, is one of their early investors. Key to their success was what happened two years before.

They believed in their product but they also needed to ensure that the product fit a larger customer set. So they set the shower head up in several gym locker rooms in the San Francisco area. Philip would then camp outside and talk to the hundreds of people who had used the shower.

In the early versions, one piece of feedback was that the water droplets didn't get warm enough. This wasn't something that the founders noticed, but there was enough feedback for them to recognize it was a potential issue. They spent an additional 12 months just on R&D to find a solution. That ended up being a key factor in the success of the Nebia crowdfunding campaign and early investors signing on.

This story illustrates the importance of relevance, which is about building an understanding beyond yourself. This can only come with customer development.

In all of these cases, a key factor for the success of the launch was in knowing the customer and co-creating with them. At the end of the day, what you are launching into, whether it's your career, your project or your business, has to be relevant. It has to address the needs of the people who you are trying to serve.

The best way to create relevance, to know the hearts and desires of your people, is to engage them. Ask them, and then listen. What are they telling you? How can you solve their problem and fulfil their desires?

Make the ability to co-create with your customers as one of your differentiators. When you do so, you significantly increase the probability for a successful launch.

CHAPTER 12
GOOD IDEAS
CAN COME
FROM
ANYWHERE

"One of the most powerful questions you can ask someone is – what do you think?"
– Brigadier General Becky Halstead (Ret)

Throughout any launch process, getting stuck is inevitable. It may be in the beginning, in coming up with an idea for launch, in encountering a seemingly insurmountable challenge or in trying to recapture the initial momentum.

Something to remember is that good ideas can come from anywhere. Two key things to bear in mind are:

- Be present so you can really see the possibilities
- Break out of labels and from hierarchies when seeking ideas from people

Wellington, a boutique investment banking firm, had appointed Bob Evans to start up the London office and to build up their Global Fixed Income Division. Bob had never built an investment team from the ground up. His inspiration for the organizational structure? Bees.

A typical beehive produces 150-200 pounds of honey in a summer – quite a feat when you consider that each bee produces the equivalent of a fingernail's worth of honey. Bob recognized the efficiency, trust, responsibility and selflessness that's inherent in beehives. This was supported by an organizational architecture that included the 'hive mind' (which has no central controlling power), a 'peer network' structure (which leads to collective decision making) and a 'swarm network' (which enables the hive's adaptivity and flexibility).

Bob explains:

"As I learned more about the structure of bees and their hive society I saw some interesting applications to the potential structure of an investment team. All major decisions are made by majority rule. The hive is a complex and non-linear structure that looks messy and chaotic from the outside but is actually incredibly efficient on the inside."

Inspired by the hive architecture and the power of bees, he created a flat, empowering and highly adaptive structure, where the team made decisions in a transparent way.

"No one has fancy titles: We're all just regular bees, buzzing around, creating a lot of chaos. Like a beehive – we want a little chaos – that's where the creativity comes from – along with the ability to adapt and be flexible. As a group, we're very comfortable with the lack of hierarchy and the focus on specialization, trust and shared responsibility."

Can the same principles of soliciting ideas from anywhere happen in an established, centuries-old institution? Can the idea of sourcing ideas more broadly across ranks also apply to military teams?

This happened to a special operations unit. Mosul, Iraq, is a city of nearly two million people. Transportation is dependent on the orange and white taxi cabs throughout the city. In 2004, al Qaida operators within the city sought to intimidate locals by rigging taxi cabs with explosives and driving them into local markets and schools. Searching every cab in the city would have been an impossible task.

The commander at that time, Brigadier Gen (now 4 Star General) Robert Brooks Brown, had created a culture of good ideas and innovation drawn from all levels of the unit. It was a type of leadership that cascaded through all units of his command.

A young American company commander had a great idea. Remove the trunk lids. His commander was supportive of the decision and he went to approach the local taxi union with the idea. The next day they started to do so and al Qaida responded by beheading one cab driver as an example.

The company commander went back to the cab union and asked what they wanted to do. The cab driver's union decided that they would not be intimidated and they accelerated their trunk removals. Within days, thousands of cabs patrolled the city without their trunk lids as a display of public defiance against al Qaida intimidation.

This success started with the leader brainstorming beyond just those with the decision-making power to include those who have the influx of information at the front lines.

Good ideas can come from anywhere. You just have to create the environment for them to encounter you and be present enough to see it when they do.

"There is nothing in a caterpillar that tells you it would turn into a butterfly."
– R Buckminster Fuller

PART THREE

IMAGINE: DISCOVER THE POSSIBLE

CHAPTER 13
PLAN FOR
LUCK

*"Look out of the window and see what
is visible but yet unseen."*
– Peter Drucker

What if luck and opportunity are all around you, but you just aren't present enough to see it? What if the door has been open all along and all you had to do is to walk through it?

My friend Sally Webb is one of the ballsiest people I know. Some people walk through doors. She leaps through and prays for a soft landing. She is also the number one events planner in the world.

In 1986, there were no events planning companies, let alone a multibillion dollar industry like today. Sally had been working in public relations, where most events planning sits. Realizing she was quite good at it, she saw an opportunity.

She met with Alan Parry, the junior deputy chairman of Lloyd's of London, the insurance company that employed her then husband. She proposed that her start-up, The Special Event Company, plan a major event for the 300th birthday celebration of the firm. He told her she could, but she would have to raise all the funding herself. To add insult to the challenge, he gave her his blunt assessment of the situation.

"You'll never do it."

Rather than deter her, this galvanized Sally. She assumed the majority of the risk and knocked on doors for sponsors. She did pull it off – and spectacularly. Parry was so impressed that he continued using her company for various events. He later became a key leader in the office of the Lord Mayor of London. From there, those events opened more doors and introductions for Sally to captains of industry and movie stars.

Was it luck that Alan would end up in government, which paved the way to more possibilities for her company? Yes, but she had to also be prepared so when that luck surfaced, she could make it happen.

Not all launches need to be on that scale. You can also plan for luck in small moments by creating conditions for it to happen. In the process, you may be lucky to discover new directions for projects. But that doesn't mean you just pursue whatever opportunities come your way.

Being intentionally opportunistic is how Mia Wise thinks about doing things with purpose, but without blinders. You don't have to be wedded to your current path. When something that captures your interest appears, you can pause and be open to pursuing it.

Mia is one of the most brilliant twenty-something year olds I've ever met. After graduation, she had planned on signing up for a data analytics job with a start-up. A chance conversation led her to deviate from her path and become an analyst at a boutique consulting firm instead. And that led her to discover one of her passions – cognitive psychology and human behaviour applied in leadership.

It wasn't a blind chase, but a deliberate and purposeful evaluation. Though the jobs were different in context, they shared a compelling thread. Mia knew she wanted a challenging work environment, an innovative opportunity to contribute in lots of ways, and be surrounded by people who would challenge her way of thinking. The intentionality anchored her decision, but how it was expressed was completely different.

She explains:

"There are a lot of people who are opportunistic and chase down everything that they see, but when you do that, you can miss an opportunity to make an impact. Being prepared for luck is not always a proactive process, but also a reactive process so when you are presented with those opportunities then you are honouring them and giving them a chance."

This goes back to the core of knowing what you value and what your values are.

Andrea Hyde beautifully sums up the futility of plotting out what you want to do, but allowing for luck, value and passion to work together:

"Figure out what your passion is, throw yourself into it, and embrace it. My career has been a real confluence of timing and meeting the right people and a lot of good luck. Part of that is throwing yourself into something and understanding if it's going to work for you. Then, figure out what's next, how you can grow and how you can give back."

Andrea had undergone a few career launches of her own. She was CEO of French Connection UK and then entered the entrepreneurial path as CEO of Burch Creative Capital. Not long after her success, she was tapped by Reese Witherspoon to start the actress's new lifestyle company, Draper James.

I remember when I asked Andrea's advice on *Thinking Cap Princesses*, a series that I was developing to empower kids as problem solvers; she shared how a big part of the launch process was devoted to figuring out who you are and who you are not.

With Draper James, her team held off pressures from investors and deliberately took a year to understand the market and what the brand was going to be in relation to that market. That intentionality empowered them to see the opportunities and know which ones to pursue and which ones not to. It allowed them to be truly prepared for luck.

BEHAVIOURAL ECONOMICS CONCEPT - PRIMING

A launch is a change, a deviation from where you currently are. Half of the challenge is for others to see themselves out of current labels and accept the potential change. For example, Iyoumay get promoted and be ready to launch into a new role. But your colleagues may still see me in the old role because the associations are there. So, how can you prime them to see you in the new promoted role?

Priming is the activation of subconscious associations that you have with a word or object just before you start a task. For example, a person who sees the word 'green' may be able to identify the word 'grass' faster. It can also refer to a psychological technique to train your memories.

Priming is getting yourself into the right frame of mind. It is also addressing how others have seen you up to now and getting away from labels.

CHAPTER 14
FIND YOUR FUN

"Fun is good."
– Dr Seuss

Something magical happens when you laugh. You become more positive. More hopeful. Something magical also happens when people share laughter. Tensions ease and you remember you are all in this together.

Because of this, you have a better chance of creating new good habits by finding the fun in the loop. Imagine trying to launch a new exercise regime, a new role at work or even just a new diet programme. All of these require you to rethink and chuck your current habits and routines and adopt new ones. The process can be gruelling, if not annoying because at its core is a behavioural change.

Yet, why do people often overlook the power of fun?

MAKE FUN A DELIVERABLE

I had expected Nicolai Schulze to be driven by efficiency when I first met him as his executive coach for the Duke Leadership Program. From Germany, he was head of corporate purchasing for indirect materials and capital goods in the EMEA region for Continental, a leading global automotive supplier. In this role, Nicolai was launching and testing new projects constantly for implementing new systems, processes, procedures or organizational structures for Continental's purchasing community on all levels. Imagine my surprise when he told me that he made fun a deliverable for every project.

Continental is a decades old company, now dealing with a multi-generational and multi-cultural workforce. Nicolai first came up with the idea when he and a colleague from IT, Markus Frieske, planned and structured a project for implementing a new IT-system for their purchasing community worldwide. They were both rather new to the corresponding areas of responsibility but they were aware that there was tension between the IT and purchasing departments due to frictions in daily operations and unsuccessful former projects.

They needed to decrease the tension between both departments in order to assure maximum outcomes during brainstorming sessions and efficiency during the working and implementation phase. Common team-building was neither sufficient nor budgeted.

"Markus and I realized quickly that we were getting along very well, laughing a lot during these prep-sessions – and this enabled us to bond easily, even though we both were 'briefed' by our corresponding departments. So, we decided that we needed to find a way to transport this to our team. And we did so by defining an additional deliverable for the project: fun.

"Most of the team members were surprised, because this was unusual. And in the beginning, they thought it might just be a joke, that we would delete it before the final presentation to management/steering. But we presented it. Management accepted it and so we kept it in our project goals."

In the beginning, Nicolai used it to justify several team dinners and activities towards management and that helped create the priming and normalizing phases. In meetings or workshops Markus and Nicolai related to their 'special deliverable' when they felt that discussions were getting too tense or unproductive.

Just by reminding the team about the deliverable to have fun, people would relax immediately, some laughing, some shaking their heads as if to say 'those two are annoying, but right'. In any case, the discussion would continue in a more open manner afterwards, delivering more output: quantity – and quality-wise. Soon, team members caught on to the fun factor and began using it in their own discussions. This resulted in one of the best collaborating and most efficient project teams in the IT/purchasing cooperation.

So, I wasn't wrong about Nicolai when I thought he was efficient. However, his efficiency came from a keen attunement to the human factor. If he was to nurture productivity and imagination, he had to nurture the souls of his team. In making fun a deliverable, his team became more meaningfully efficient for any launch project they embarked on.

One caveat: Sometimes, in the beginning, team members might see this as a wild-card for not working seriously ... but that is where leaders have to explain and clearly define limits and expectations.

There's another benefit – when you intentionally build joy and fun into the process, you are hedging towards a positive experience, regardless of the outcome. And fun doesn't have to be just project based. It can permeate the entire culture of the company.

INJECT FUN INTO EVERYTHING

Fun is also critical beyond the company. It can be a core factor to building and propelling a movement forward. If you were walking through downtown Durham, North Carolina, chances are you'd spot stickers with giant squiggles and the tag '#artstigators'.

More than a dozen Durham restaurants feature menu items with an Artstigator scribble to celebrate the Crazies for the Arts. These culinary arts collaborations are the brainchild of Amy Unell, arts engagement maven at Duke University. Amy has helped sprinkle fun throughout the campus and the city, and has launched a movement that bursts the arts into a community around creativity, the #artstigators.

Launch is in Amy's DNA. I first met her when she was the Emmy-nominated producer of NBC's *Today Show*. She had launched her own production company and directed a documentary about Olympic coach, Al Buehler. She was about to embark on a new adventure at Duke – one that drew on her passions for teaching, for the arts, for innovation and for community-building.

The Artstigators idea originated from a conversation she had with screen printing artist Bill Fick about making arts and creativity accessible, inclusive and fun. Artstigators clicked the moment Monuts (a local gourmet donuts shop) made a special donut with dark chocolate drizzle as the squiggle logo.

Amy shares:

"Fun is at the heart of Artstigatin'. There's no one way or right way to instigate art, it's up to the Artstigator!"

Injecting fun into the movement was key to its success. Besides local restaurants, student and community organizations team up with #artstigators on events, pop-ups and projects to help amplify and spread the word about creative opportunities at Duke and beyond. This has resulted in other fun-filled outputs.

Actors Rob Lowe, Retta and Ben Folds each filmed spontaneous and fun 'Artstigator Minute' videos declaring how they each 'artstigate'. This helped spark the movement beyond Durham. The movement has over 3,000 instagram followers from Durham to Denver to Brazil.

ENABLE THE CHANGE BY DISCOVERING THE FUN

Fun can also enable you to more ably change, even when the situation surfaces unexpected challenges. An example can be seen in the experiences of John Allison, who had been at BB&T, a major bank in North Carolina, for 28 years. He had led the bank through the subprime mortgage crisis of 2008, launched a BB&T Leadership University, and then retired as CEO and became chairman.

Like many who were corporate executives (especially CEOs) with a built-in support infrastructure, the retirement move came with challenges to his identity in the context of relevance and power. He also had an organization full of bright people who he could delegate to and have the confidence that projects and ideas could move forward.

He discovered the key was to have a new sense of purpose. Shortly after retirement, he was recruited to run CATO, a free market think tank in Washington DC, which he saw as another adventure.

"If I had stayed under BB&T, I would have had less fun, not because it wasn't very challenging, not because I wouldn't have had a lot of interface there. But, doing something pretty radically different like becoming a college professor and then running a free market think tank in Washington DC, enlightened and broadened my whole perception of the world in a way that you can never get in one industry."

When I last spoke with John, he had retired from CATO and is on his next adventure. He told me that he is now travelling the world and having fun with his wife.

So, make sure you make fun a deliverable and incorporate it into your culture, into your world view. When you do so, not only are you going to have a more enjoyable experience, but you are also going to be more productive, more engaged and more likely to encounter imagination touch points. By injecting fun in the process, not only will you become more motivated, but you will also have a more meaningful launch journey.

BEHAVIOURAL ECONOMICS CONCEPT - ENVIRONMENT MATTERS

Our surroundings matter

How do we get irrationally creative? At a conference for behavioural and health scientists to explore how to help people make healthier choices, something interesting happened. Trays of cookies offered outside the conference room were immediately devoured by the same individuals vowing to battle such irrational, unhealthy choices. The key to eating healthy isn't to put the cookie in front of you and then try to resist it (as your stomach dismisses the rational logic your brain concocts). The key is to not have cookies in front of you at all. Today, there are so many facets of life competing for your commitment/loyalty – they are the conference rooms. Each of these rooms holds detractors and projectors to your goals. An environment that holds more inspiration than distractions can go a long way in helping you reach your goals. The occurrence of irrational choice may have more to do with the environment you work in than the cookies that tempt you. When you build a healthy environment conducive to supporting your goals, you face fewer cookies along the way. So how can you make your surroundings conducive to irrational creativity?

Exercise:

Is there a song that makes you feel like you can conquer the world? Play this when you are feeling down.

Is there a place within walking distance that inspires you? Walk there to hang out for a while and think through the challenges you are working on.

CHAPTER 15
GOING FOR IT

> "Two roads diverged in a wood, and I –
> I took the one less travelled by."
> – Robert Frost

In Robert Frost's poem, *The Road Not Taken*, there are two roads which diverge in a yellow wood. Being one traveller, he stands long, thinking about which road to take and is sorry that he cannot travel down both. In your launch story, one road is to move forward in a different direction; the other is to stay on the same path. And it doesn't have to always be the road less taken.

Sometimes you can get stuck in the decision-making process. To launch or not to launch? To go or not to go? And where you are usually stuck is in the absence of data – about the uncertainty, the consequences of taking one path over another. Sometimes, taking a step forward can unfurl new data on how the rest of the world reacts and how you react yourself.

Darren Eales experienced a sideways move in his launch into a sports executive career. A professional football player, he came to the United States from England and was drafted into a new league. When an injury prevented him from playing, he returned to England, earned a law degree from Cambridge and practised as a barrister for six years. Though he was successful, he didn't enjoy it. At his core, he was a team player and needed a career that brought a sense of team, similar to when he had been playing sports.

Then he noticed a potential opportunity. The Glazers had just bought Manchester United and one of their first actions was to hire a legal counsel, something that was out of the norm at the time for a club. He applied for it and though he didn't get the job because he was five years short of the required 10-year experience, he realized something. Whatever Manchester United was doing, other clubs would also follow.

Instead of waiting for other clubs to follow suit, he became more proactive. He wrote to other clubs and told them that if they were considering doing what Manchester United had done, he would be interested in having a chat with them. He received 15 rejections, but then received a call from two clubs. One of them offered him a job and he launched into a new career as a sports executive.

"You have to take the risk. I knew this would give me a chance to do what I loved, and that was important to me. I went in (with West Bromwich Albion) as legal counsel and in about a year, I switched to director of football. So I was running the football side, but it gave me an in into the front office, and then clearly having a legal background is massively important for all the player contracts and the global nature of the game."

After 4 ½ seasons with smaller but well-run clubs, he received the job at Tottenham Hotspur, which is one of the top clubs in the Premier League. During his tenure, he was voted chairman of the FA cup (which is the English soccer equivalent to the Super Bowl).

A few years ago Darren took another risk. He decided to leave Tottenham and went to the United States to start up an entirely new team – Atlanta United – in the new Major League Soccer. In his early 40s, Darren is already shaping the new sports league. Just because something hasn't been done before, doesn't mean it has to be done the same way. Sometimes, going for it not only requires understanding the risks, but seeing the big win.

Kafui Dzirasa is one of the most prominent young scientists of our time with dual MD and PhD degrees. His work on understanding neuro-transmissions and rewiring to address mental illness has garnered him many grants and accolades, including the White House Young Scientists Award. I first met him when I was giving a speech for the National Student Medical Association, where he was serving as president while completing his medical training.

A few years ago, he took a daring new path in physician scientist training. Most of the time, there is a scientific training gap when those pursuing MD PhDs enter residency. The consequence is a delay in the person's research career and the pathway to funding. What if there's a way that they can create a medical residency that would also allow for engagement in part-time research? At that time Kafui, with three of his mentors, the senior vice chancellor of the medical school, the former department chair of psychiatry and the former director of the National Institute of Mental Health, decided to test out a new paradigm for training.

He shares:

"The goal at that point in time was not to see if it was scalable, it was just to figure out if it was feasible, as a pilot experiment. So I, in my late 20s, was a bit of a glutton for punishment, and I always found that I worked best outside of normal paradigm. I thought it was the only type of system in which I could have done residency because I loved being in the lab."

The goal of the experiment was to keep him publishing while he finished up his residency so he could quickly launch his independent research career and position him for grant applications right after residency. It was a major risk. But Kafui went for it. Why? Core to him being Kafui is an orientation for innovation.

"In 2009, my orientation was going after massive ideas and chasing after them, despite whether people thought that they would work or not."

Influenced by his graduate mentor, whose goal was to make paralyzed people walk again, he started growing up as a scientist, with an orientation towards the impossible, and not shying away from it. Another influence was his longstanding mentor, Freeman Hrabowski, president at the University of Maryland, who decided in the late 80s that he was going to create a programme which increased the number of African Americans getting PhDs in the sciences. It is now the number one producer of African Americans going off to get MD PhDs and probably in the top two in terms of PhDs in the country.

Due to its success, NIH became really interested in this model. It's now trying to create new grant mechanisms to support physician scientists across the country doing similar sorts of innovations in training. By 'going for it', Kafui also opened up the pathway for those behind him.

So why don't you go for it more often? The main reason might be paralysis because of the number of choices before you.

BEHAVIOURAL ECONOMICS CONCEPT - CHOICE PARADOX

Recently, a student shared her stress of 'fear of missing out' (FOMO) with me. She had entered the recruitment process, intending to look at social entrepreneurship or consulting jobs. When she found other classmates pursuing options in marketing, finance and myriad other possibilities, she became worried she might be limiting herself. To gain perspective, I offered her an analogy.

Imagine you are going to a dessert shop and the only decision you plan on making is between a banana split and a slice of Oreo cake. You will be happy with either one. But when you enter the store, you see options from mango ice cream to pistachio macarons, to tonnes of other possibilities you had never imagined. You are now overwhelmed and stressed by the choices when you would have been just as happy with your original two choices. Can you focus back on those two? However, if the opportunity arises and the person across the counter offers you a free sample of strawberry cupcake, assuming you like strawberries, that doesn't mean you shouldn't try it.

Sometimes, we get paralyzed by the number of decisions and possibilities. This is normal – it's choice paradox. Choice or analysis paralysis results when you overthink a situation to the point that you never take an action. When overwhelmed by a perception of too many decisions, your default is to try for the perfect solution rather than making a choice and then pivoting if needed.

In choice paradox, the costs of time and effort into making what you think is the perfect decision (if such a thing were possible), far outweighs the benefits.

One of the easiest ways to simplify that process is to have a good understanding of who you are. So, if you know who you are, you can simplify the question from, 'is this a good idea?' – and you are going to have a million good ideas – to, 'is this me?' That's the decision heuristic you should be using throughout the launch process.

In the launch process, there may be opportunities that come up and it's easy to want to jump down each rabbit hole and explore. There is a phase for being open minded. However, if you are not careful and get lost in deciding which rabbit hole to explore, you may get side-tracked and end up not going down any, or be no happier in jumping down one after going through the stress of deciding, than the one you had originally intended. How can you straddle the line between open-minded possibilities and choice paradox? The key is knowing who you are. 'Is this me,' is an easier question to answer than, 'Is this a good opportunity?' or 'Is this a good direction?'

CHAPTER 16
BRILLIANT
FAILURES

"I have not failed. I've just found 10,000 ways that won't work."
– Thomas Edison

Imagine you have a choice to take a class. It's a great class. You'll learn a lot that will help you succeed. But you also know that no matter how hard you work, the chance of you getting above 40% is pretty slim. Would you still take the class?

For many entering the launch process, that's the type of question you will face. Are you willing to risk that type of failure rate? Would you risk feeling embarrassed?

Melissa Bernstein not only takes the 40% success rate; she also celebrates the 60% failure rate. In Melissa's office, on a wall behind her desk, are some 500 of her favourite toys. Melissa is the co-founder and chief toy designer of Melissa & Doug's, a multi-million dollar toy company that she launched with her sweetheart 28 years ago. What's fascinating is that these toys have all bombed in the market place. There were lots more. These were just the 10% that could fit into the space.

When you think about it, more of what she's created has failed than succeeded.

"You really can't view them as failures. They are just part of the journey. I was the biggest perfectionist and most fearful of failure of any person on the planet.

"The reason we have been successful is we never stop failing and creating. The more you worry about having that failure, the less you will create. The lower your chance of success will be. If it's a percentage, you have to keep failing in order to keep succeeding."

Those 'failed' toys are also a visual inspiration to her every day.

"If you have the courage to look at your failures and see them for what they are, and really understand them and why they didn't work, you won't see them as failures at all. You'll see them as amazing launch pads for discovery and lessons that lead you to operate differently going forward."

Today, Melissa & Doug toys are loved by children in more than 80 countries around the world.

A failure can also launch you to different paths if you know how to pivot and let go a little bit. I define it as having a different outcome to what you had anticipated or hoped for. And often, it's about circumstances not of your own doing, but out of your control. You can do everything 'right', put in your best effort, but due to timing or a different competitive field, still fail.

Deb James had always wanted to be a diplomat. To prepare, she majored in Comparative Areas Studies and minored in Spanish and then pursued a Master's degree in International Affairs. Armed with degrees from top schools and an all-star resume, she moved to Washington DC and applied for a diplomat officer position in the United States Foreign Service. And did not get it!

"I was devastated and literally cried for three or four days. After my 'pity party', reality set in. I needed a job, a means of livelihood, and a pay check. I needed to start looking for whatever was next. So, I applied everywhere else I could think of in the federal government because I still wanted to work in public service."

She entered the US Department of the Army as a civilian. Although it wasn't her dream job, she soon grew to love the work because she felt like she was making a contribution and her work on national security issues mattered. This was a different path, but it was still aligned with the original reason why she wanted to be a diplomat. Her work and ensuing 34 years have grown even more about mission, purpose, people and mentorship.

"Life will not turn out as you plan or as you wish. You will be thrown curveballs, both personally and professionally. The most important thing is if you do fall down, make sure you know you can get back up again. You may need a period to grieve, where you need to cry or feel regretful, but you need to keep going.

"Whatever door shuts here; another will open up over there. Maybe it wasn't your original plan, but that doesn't mean it can't be a fantastic plan. So, you need to go for it, and walk through that door and seize that opportunity.

"So, I look back on it now, and I'm actually grateful that the foreign service didn't pick me so many years ago, because if they had done so, I can't imagine that I would have had a better career than the one I've had in Defence."

Until January 2017, Deb James was the Secretary of the United States Air Force, one of the highest-ranking civilians overseeing a military service branch. She was responsible for more than 660,000 active-duty airmen and their families and for overseeing the Air Force's annual budget of more than $139 billion.

Failure can also help you discover something unexpected about yourself – that you might be braver than you think. Failure is also a tremendous opportunity for reflection and teaches you valuable lessons about yourself – that you don't have to be 100% perfect 100% percent of the time. That you can go out of the confines of what you previously imagined and fly. It can lead to new insights and be a great building block for your next launch. If you have a new relationship with failure, just imagine what you might be able to do!

BEHAVIOURAL ECONOMICS PRINCIPLE - GOAL GRADIENT THEORY

You can think you are closer to reaching your goals even though, in reality, you may be no further to the end than before. With goal gradient theory, the closer you think you are to achieving something, the more motivated you are to complete it.

What this means is you can motivate yourself to break down a larger goal into smaller concrete goals. And then chart your progress. Each step you take towards the goal will deepen your sense of commitment. You can also trick yourself to becoming more motivated if you frame your journey not as starting at zero, but with some steps completed. Charting is key because if you don't perceive yourself as progressing, you may be demotivated to continue.

CHAPTER 17
QUESTIONS
IN SEARCH
OF ANSWERS

*"I was born not knowing and have had only
a little time to change that here and there."*
– Richard Feynman

One of the major obstacles when launching anything is a fear of the unknown. A fear of not knowing, not having all the answers, not knowing how to do something. Sometimes you can lean on this fear as reason enough not to start the launch process.

This is especially endemic among those who pursue perfection. When I was in my twenties, I would sometimes fear trying something because I was worried I wouldn't be good at it. At those moments, a very wise friend, Kate Neubert, reminded me, *"When you were born, did you know how to walk? Well, now, you can walk, run, leap."*

I don't think anyone can remember when they started walking and the number of stumbles and falls to get to this point. You took those first steps before you were fearful of the unknown, of the not knowing. You saw others around you walking and wanted to walk too.

What if you can get back to this mindset? And see that becoming good is just a matter of time? And between now and then, is just a series of trying, stumbling, learning and becoming better and better?

A story that illustrates this learning mindset in relation to time comes from a session with Cathy Englebert, CEO of Deloitte and Janet Foutty, CEO of Deloitte Consulting. We were at the Deloitte Women's Leadership Launch, which I was invited to participate in as an academic luminary.

A year before, Cathy had approached Janet to consider putting her name in the running for the next CEO of consulting and gave her an honest assessment.

"You are not ready now. But what do we have to do to prepare you to be ready nine months from now?"

There were no guarantees that she would get the job. But the guarantee was that she would be ready for the job.

I had a 'eureka' moment then. So many people I know (including myself) have the imposter syndrome. It's this fear of being found out, a pervasive belief that you are not qualified for the position or accolade. It's a feeling of being a fraud. It affects everyone including the greats. Maya Angelou, one of the greatest writers of our times, once said, *"After seven novels, I am afraid of being found out I'm not a good writer."*

So this means that every great CEO, every great writer, great runner, at one point was unqualified for that role. Becoming qualified was a matter of being prepared and a matter of time.

Why should it matter? All right, if that were true, that you aren't qualified now because of what you don't know, let's move forward and figure out how to be qualified. Isn't being qualified only a matter of time, if you take on the mindset of being questions in search of answers?

It's said that careers of great ambition are also careers of great anxiety. With this mindset, you can take the anxiety out of the equation. Furthermore, what if you view those questions that you have – evidence of your knowledge gap – what if they can become an asset rather than a liability?

One of the quickest ways to build a relationship is to ask a question and sincerely seek an answer. It's a great way to build allies and expand your network of champions.

Alan Mulally had been at Boeing for 37 years of his career. All he had ever known was planes. Then he became CEO of Ford, the first outsider to take that role. The company was going to hit $17 billion in losses that year. The stock was at $1.18/share. The company was also highly decentralized with each region around the world doing their own thing. Alan was undaunted because he knew the answers to the turnarounds existed within the company. If he was going to launch this turnaround, he had to encourage people to tell the truth about their problems so they could collectively come up with the answers. As a start, he pulled the entire leadership team together from around the world for weekly Business Plan Review (BPR) meetings. Many of the team had not worked together before.

When they were together, he had a reporting system. Each leader had objectives which they marked Green (great); Yellow (in the works); Red (problem). At that time, Ford had a culture where people hid issues. The first week, every report was green. Same with weeks 2, 3 and 4. Alan had joined in September. Ford had a projected $17 billion annual loss by December.

Finally, Mark Fields, who headed up the Canadian region, had the courage to indicate a Red on his report. He had run into an issue and didn't have the answers. Rather than chastising him as all the other executives expected, Alan celebrated the Red. They were now openly confronting their challenges head on.

He told Mark, *"I don't know the answer either. But it's OK. We are going to figure it out together."* And they did. The other executives around the table piped up to offer resources and solutions that soon sent Mark's report on the way to Green. They became more open about the challenges they faced and more comfortable with not knowing the answers, but having confidence that together, they could find the solutions.

Week by week, month by month, Alan built the team and changed the culture through relentless execution of process and disciplined behaviour. By the time he left, the stock price was at $18/share and he was ranked one of the top leaders in the world. And today, Mark Fields is Alan's successor as Ford CEO.

No launch is ever done alone. Alan knew that. In this case, they were all questions in search of answers. The team had the answers. They just had to unlock them. Together.

---

1 Adapted "The 6 Types of Questions Great Leaders Ask" by Sanyin Siang in Forbes and World Economic Forum April 1, 2015

USING QUESTIONS THROUGH THE LAUNCH PROCESS[1]

When launching a project or a business, you may be dealing with a rapidly shifting marketplace, and complicated and complex sets of issues. It's nearly impossible for any one person to have the full deck of data, knowledge and experience to define the issues and generate the most effective solutions.

So, key to launch is surrounding yourself with those who have knowledge, expertise or points of views that you don't possess. Among those you are bringing into your tribe, you have to surface key levers and drivers among viewpoints that may be in tension with one another in order to inform a strategy, direction or decision.

It's alright not to have the answers at the onset. So how can you lean on the power of questions to see beyond your current opportunities and challenges and truly draw on the insights of those who you are bringing into your launch journey? Often the most innovative ideas result from questions that reframe an issue or unearth new possibilities.

Here are five ways you can use questions:

1. **Drive to the heart of an issue.**
The 'why' question – you can ask questions that probe and filter out the critical from the noise, paint the complete picture, and connect the dots. Take a step back and ask whether the current framing is the best way to engage the issue. Why is this the case? How does this affect us? What are we assuming? What do we need to know that we

don't yet know? What other questions do we need to be asking right now? These types of questions unleash the collective wisdom of a group to truly define a problem or opportunity. What are some guiding principles you think through when formulating good questions?

Find questions that get to the motivation of something. Once you understand why people are doing something, it creates a context for you to look at it from their lens and a different point of view.

2. Create a collective sense of ownership and foster collaboration.

The 'what do you' think question – well-constructed questions can resolve the tension of seemingly opposing viewpoints, as well as getting people excited and more engaged in a process. Hence, you can lean on questions among your launch team to facilitate a collaborative approach and integrative thinking. Applied to launch, you can use questions to invite people into the conversation and start creating and building your tribe and fierce advocates.

3. Fire up the imagination.

The 'what if' question – this is especially needed today when un-certainty and bad news plague even the best of organizations. Madison Avenue legend, Keith Reinhard, Chairman Emeritus, DDB Worldwide, once recounted the story of what happened when DDB lost the American Airlines (AA) account. The news dealt a major blow to employee morale.

So, on that day, Keith asked, *"If you were to write the headline for the DDB and the AA relationship five years from now, what would that headline be?"* By asking a question that ignited his employees' imagination, he also rekindled a sense of optimism. In the end, his team came up with ideas that enabled them to win back the AA account.

4. Establish Credibility and convey who you are.
The well-framed question – this can highlight the understanding of an issue and represent the questioner's point of view or set of values. Think about great interviewers and the nature of the questions that they ask and what these convey to us about them – both their areas of expertise as well as their values.

5. Create reflection.
Because of the discovery nature of the launch process, questions are especially important for personal reflection. You are going to go through a range of emotions in the launch process – be attuned to how you are feeling and ask why you feel that way. Be present and don't be afraid to challenge yourself with questions you may not want to hear.

While this section talks about the types of questions you should ask, a key point to remember is that the types of questions you ask may differ from context to context for each launch. Make sure that you are asking different questions than the ones those in your tribe are used to hearing, which can shift how they approach the problem.

And finally, what's the key to asking good questions so you can maximize their potential? Listening. There is no point in asking a question if you are not going to listen. That would be a terrible waste of everyone's time, including your own.

"Next play."
– Mike Krzyzewski after every single play
in his basketball games.

PART FOUR

NEXT PLAY

CHAPTER 18 PIVOTS AND REFRAMES

"Change can be frightening, and the temptation is often to resist it. But change almost always provides opportunities – to learn new things, to rethink tired processes, and to improve the way we work."
– Klaus Schwab

Recently, Wendy Kuran, a former mentor and boss, invited me to give a talk on storytelling and creating a family legacy for a course she was directing for a group of high-level Chinese family business leaders. That's how I met Liu Yongxing, one of China's first billionaires.

Mr Liu was a former factory worker who couldn't afford to buy his young son a piece of meat during Festival Season. He was good at fixing radios and, together with his two brothers, he collected enough money to start a quail business. His region, Gujia, became the quail capital of China.

He then went to the US on a study tour. He told us how, in Pittsburgh, he saw the steel mills and the consequences and possibilities of industrialization. When he returned home, he knew they could be bigger by pivoting into new industries. The three brothers split into three different companies, with Mr Liu creating the East Hope Company. The company invested in aluminium, chemicals and, nowadays, in solar power. Mr Liu's pivots for the company paid off. Today, he is worth more than $6 billion.

What he demonstrated in this story is something I've seen many successful launchers do. They can move forward with an idea, but through intentional engagement with others and with a constant mindset oriented towards discovery, they reframe the original ideas and pivot where needed. In Mr Liu's case, he pivoted the original business from a quail feed company into a much larger enterprise without losing sight of the core mission.

We also saw this in the American company GE. More than a hundred years old, GE was undergoing its own pivot to become a hybrid company that sits at the intersection of physical and digital. This required a shift in internal mindsets and a re-examination of existing behaviours. GE Chief Marketing Officer, Linda Boff, shared their thinking with me:

"Part of turning the ship when the ship is as big as we are, and as venerable (124 years is venerable), you get good at doing things a certain way. What's been interesting and challenging, is that some of what has made us so good at being a manufacturer, being a company that knows how to operate its scale, how to operate in nearly 200 countries around the world, are not necessarily the same things that make you good in the digital era.

"Ideally you don't fail but if you're going to fail, pivot and learn from what you know, moving at the speed of the market—and we

developed from that this idea that we call Fastworks. It's really a way of working, and has become kind of shorthand for the way that we're trying to work with fewer layers, less bureaucracy. I think you can't transform a company externally if you're not transforming it internally."

Early on, it may not be a pivot, but rather a reframe. I've noticed that a common mistake made by start-ups is defining the problem they are trying to solve either too broadly or too narrowly. How a problem is framed can prime those working on it to think about possibilities and constraints in new ways.

Sometimes the pivot and reframing is internal. It happens in the structuring to accomplish the same end goal, while leveraging distinctive strengths. David Robinson is a basketball legend. By the time he retired, he had won two NBA championships, two Olympic medals and is a member of the basketball Hall of Fame. A graduate of the US Naval Academy, David always had a heart for service and positive impact. Early on, he created the Carver Academy to help provide education to underserved minorities in Texas. But soon hit a problem with scaling.

He posed the scaling challenge as part of a practicum course for MBA students. That's how David met Daniel Bassichis, who along with his classmates, proposed a novel idea. Why not create a for-profit entity that leveraged David's character and celebrity with a focus on strong ethical practices? And then, donate 10% of the profits into the non-profit and social good that was David's passion.

This idea reframed the structure of David's lifelong pursuit into Admiral Capital Group, a private equity firm managing hundreds of millions of real estate assets. They use every asset they invest to create opportunities for lower income communities. 10% of the profits go into the Admiral Center, a non-profit that partners with the Gates Foundation and other top foundations to provide funding for education. And as a case of embracing different, Daniel came in as a partner with David on Admiral Capital Group.

The ability to pivot and reframe applies to career launch processes too. When I asked Edith Cooper, Partner and Global Head of Human Capital Managemetn at Goldman Sachs, about pivots, she responded:

"Your ability to 'pivot' impacts whether you're able to capture and make the most of the opportunities in front of you. However, it's important not to get caught up in the concern of 'going left' versus 'going right'. If you're over thinking every move and anxious about which direction to take, you'll end up slowing yourself down. Pivoting should be less about making the right or wrong move, and more about transitioning from one experience to the next – because after you've pieced together enough positive, meaningful and challenging experiences, that is when you see growth and begin to march towards the next level. Whether you're a new hire or a seasoned professional, it's important to regularly take a step back and evaluate yourself – what are you good at, and what should you be doing differently? Being self-aware and understanding your strengths and developmental areas will help you think through those pivotal moments as they come your way."

BEHAVIOURAL ECONOMICS CONCEPT - LOSS AVERSION

When given the choice, people have a tendency to stick to the status quo, which can get in the way of any launch. A way of managing this is leaning on another human tendency – loss aversion, one of the most powerful motivators there is. You feel losses more strongly than gains. Hence, you are likely to exert more energy to avoid a loss than to gain. So, a technique is to trick yourself into feeling like you lose if you don't move. For example, you can set up choices between a choice of loss and a choice of gain.

You can 'write an apology email' or start on the next step of your launch process.

You can put money in a jar or start on the next step of your launch process.

Not eating dessert or spending 30 minutes not doing anything other than working on your launch process and eating dessert.

You will also want to remove as many barriers to the habit as possible. So, if you are launching a new exercise regime in the morning, your workout clothes should already be laid out.

TAKE AWAYS:

■ Don't be too tied to the initial idea. Once you've anchored it around values and mission, give it room to evolve according to what's relevant and what opportunities may come your way.

■ In the beginning, how you frame an idea is key to priming the mind for what's possible and removing false constraints.

■ That reframe can happen not only in conceptualization, but also in how you structure or restructure your organization to accomplish your goals.

■ Pivots are critical in careers too. Patience and a learning and discovery mindset are key to enabling this.

CHAPTER 19
TIMING

"There were decisions in my past in which I had to accurately time in terms of understanding the difference between chronological time and the right time."
– Marty Dempsey, 18th Chairman of Joint Chiefs of Staff

Why is it that people focus so much on the outcome and forget the journey? When it's seen as a discovery process, the launch process may have more to offer than the outcome. So why is there a rush to the outcome and you see it as the sole metric for success? The danger in doing this is that you forget to give ideas the room to breathe, and yourself the space to grow.

TIMING MATTERS
Sometimes, the launch process can take longer than the anticipated period of time. I think of ideas on the shelf in search of the right time, perspective, and team.

Let's go back to Melissa Bernstein, the chief toy designer of Melissa & Doug's and her trove of failed toys behind her desk. What she's discovered is that some toys that had initially failed, were later re-launched successfully.

An example is the wooden baby products line. The first launch failed because customers were worried about keeping wooden versus plastic toys clean. But ten years later, when organic and natural became a trend, they relaunched the line with packaging tweaks and they became a success. So, what made her come back to the toy instead of discarding the line when it failed initially?

"I believed in it. I put it behind me because I still think it's watching me. And always saying – hey, remember me? I may not be working right now, but if you look at me in a little while, I might look different to you. Discovery is seeing what everyone is seeing, but thinking what no one has thought.

"Every day, I see things differently. We grow every day and our perspective changes and if we allow our minds to be fluid, who knows what we might think about the same thing tomorrow. I love that aspect of creativity, which is if you are a fluid thinker, you can always be iterative by seeing things differently as time progresses."

So what is the guiding principle for knowing the difference between something that shouldn't be introduced versus something that is worthy of belief? She responds, *"If you have a compass and the tenets by which you create something never changes."*

CHOICES ARE DYNAMIC

All of this illustrates a dynamic relationship with time. You need to stop looking at choices as static and that the circumstances won't change or that you yourself won't evolve. Often when you are evaluating someone else's successful path or looking at best practices, you tend to look at their successes and work backwards.

Kathleen Taylor has this advice to offer:

"Success when viewed in the rear-view mirror looks like it was achieved with flawless execution. But the truth of the matter is that that never happens – in life, in sports, in anything. While you're experimenting with likes and dislikes in your career, remember there is probably not much that you will do in decision making around opportunity and pivoting in your early career that will have any impact on the long-term trajectory of your life."

Kathleen has spent the majority of her career in the hospitality industry and retired as the CEO of Four Seasons. She then launched into another new chapter. Having also served for years on the Royal Bank of Canada board of directors, she became the first female to chair a major Canadian Bank in 2015. Under her leadership, RBC exceeded market expectations, earning $2.5 billion each quarter.

"People have trouble with that because usually they are choosing between this company versus that company, this city versus that city, this industry versus that industry. The truth of the matter is – there are no bad choices as long as they are thoughtfully made and they are adjusted. So many kids these days worry what happens if they choose something and they don't like it. If you don't like it, then you go do something else, go to another company. They could do anything! It's very obvious to me that this feeling of risk aversion is super high."

CHAPTER 20
BELIEF

*"When you believe something can be done,
really believe, your mind will find the ways to do it.
Believing a solution paves the way to solution."*
– David J Schwartz

Throughout the launch process, you will encounter a lot of ups and downs. What keeps you going, and ultimately takes you to the point of launch and beyond, is belief. If it's a checklist, if it's not aligned with your values, in timber with your resonant frequency, then it's going to be a lot harder to believe in as you push it forward.

Shelly Lazarus is one of the most pragmatic and thought-provoking leaders I've ever met. She is Chairman Emeritus of Ogilvy & Mather and sits on the boards of GE and the World Wildlife Federation. I walk away from every interaction with her with learning something that instantly makes me a more effective leader. With no aspiration to become CEO, her ability to turnaround tough challenges was noticed by those at the highest levels. Hence, when the New York Office of Ogilvy & Mather was undergoing a particularly tough period, Martin Sorrell, the firm's chairman, asked for her help. It was a seemingly impossible challenge to undertake. Revenues were falling. It seemed that every other day they were losing a client, and everyone of value had their résumés on the street and were willing to leave.

When I asked Shelly what led her to decide such a tough challenge, she responded:

"They needed me. The New York office is where I had come from, and where I had worked most of my time at Ogilvy. I was gone three to four years, and was surprised to see when I came back, it was all the same people. I knew them, and I knew how capable they were. They had just lost their direction and had too much failure, which is difficult for anyone to deal with.

"I knew the clients, and I knew they were good people. I knew that if we could get them to believe, we had the capacity, and the desire, to do great work. If we could do that, I knew the clients would want to stay or come back, and if not, we could win new clients. I believed it could be done."

The theme of belief continued.

"They were failing over and over again, so the first thing I had to do was to get them to believe it was possible to succeed. That was the hardest thing of all – in the midst of all the bad news, I had to get hundreds of people to believe it was possible to turn things around. I learned a lot doing it. When the problem seems too overwhelming, and people don't think they can solve it, they leave, because why even try when it doesn't seem possible?"

As a first step, she divided the problem into bite-size chunks. Instead of asking the team to take on the overwhelming goal of making the office successful, she asked whether they could make individual campaigns a little bit better.

"If you can get 25 people, give them the right individual assignments, and things they can do, you can get them to believe again. So, we set out to do small things, where we thought we could succeed, and when we did, we would celebrate. I created a rewards pool for those who were successful at meeting goals, and it worked.

"When you're in the rhythm of failure, it can be debilitating. You have to break people out of it. You've got to set out to do small things where you believe you can succeed, then you celebrate."

Do you believe in the idea to the extent you are willing to risk your job? Not all launch decisions are as dramatic as this one. However, the decision to pursue a launch comes with trade-offs in time, in money, in attention. For it to maintain your attention and energy, it has to be something that goes deeper than a checklist, but something that you believe is so worthwhile that you are willing to give up some other things.

Your belief can also determine whether you launch or not. Throughout this book, it's been about the process. The ideal outcome may not be to launch. When is such a case? When it is misaligned with your belief.

Mike Heisley,[1] the son of a train operator, emerged from a blue-collar background to become a billionaire, owner of the Memphis Grizzlies and patron of St. Jude's Children's Hospital, among countless other accomplishments. He was someone who embodied the societal definition of success.

Early in his career, after many failed deals and with deep personal investment, he finally had a breakthrough. He had a deal to purchase a stainless-steel plate manufacturing company for 25 cents on the dollar and sell it for a $100 million profit. The deal was his by legal right.

During the waiting period before closing, the owners of the company approached him and asked if he could walk away from the deal. There was another company, they explained, that had offered to buy them for 100 cents on the dollar and could keep the entire mill open, enabling the employees and town to maintain their livelihoods. But Mike would have to walk away from the deal.

Mike had a moral dilemma. So, he went home to talk it over with his dad. After hearing the pros and cons, his dad looked at Mike and said:

"Son, it looks like to me there are two opportunities here – if this steel company comes in, the creditors get 100% of their money, and 100% of the employees go back to work, and the suppliers have got much bigger business, and you get nothing.

"On the other hand, if you get the business, the creditors get screwed, 50% of the employees and their families are without work,

1 Excerpted from "The $100 Million Choice" by Sanyin Siang Huffington Post January 25, 2015

and the suppliers have their business cut in half, but you're doing good. I think I raised you better."

So Mike, who grew up poor, walked away and did not launch the deal. Two weeks after he walked away from the deal, Mike received a call from one of the biggest lenders in the country. They were so impressed with his character and told Mike that he was the type of guy they wanted to do business with. Fast forward years later, when Mike examined his billion-dollar holding company, 75% of the businesses in it were in one way or another connected with that lender.

In the end, how you engage in the process to launch, the decision to launch or not launch will be a reflection of who you are.

For me, writing this book is taking time away from my family. However, I know it won't be forever and there is a deadline, an end in sight. And what I look to is that someday, my children will be able to take this book off the shelves and read stories and insights that may help them in their launch process.

I believe in the ideas in this book and the wisdom shared by so many. I believe that this book will help readers see themselves differently after reading. Every launch is part of your legacy, whether you believe it or not. It's the mark that you leave on the people, the places and the organizations that you touch. So, how you engage in the process to launch and the decision to launch or not launch will be a reflection of who you are. It will signal your values and what you believe in to the world.

BEHAVIOURAL ECONOMICS CONCEPT - PRE-COMMITMENT

People make future decisions that are in line with decisions they have made in the past. It's because they want to believe they made the original decisions for a reason. When you put something in your own handwriting, you're far more likely to see it through than when you see a commitment that you simply check off a list. Seeing an intention or statement written by you takes it from the abstract and makes it more personal and linked to your identity. For example, research has shown that if you fill out your own doctor reminder card, you are 18% more likely to show up.

Exercise:
Write this down in your own handwriting

I can do this.
I know how to do this.
I am surrounded by people who are invested in my success.

CHAPTER 21
BE YOUR
BEST YOU

"We are not yet what we shall be, but we are growing toward it, the process is not yet finished, but it is going on, this is not the end, but it is the road."
– Martin Luther

Christopher Wren once asked three labourers on a construction site what they were doing.

The first responded with, *"I'm breaking stone."*
The second with, *"I'm making our living."*
The third with, *"I'm building a cathedral."*

While all three were critical, the answer 'building a cathedral' was the one that was most inspiring and one that shouldn't be lost sight of. In the context of the launch process, what is the equivalent of building a cathedral?

It's becoming your best you.

If every launch is an expression of who you are, then every launch process is in pursuit of becoming your best self.

A few years ago, Shep Moyle launched into the party supply business to head up Shindigz, now one of the world's largest party-supply stores. At that time, the company focused on prom programmes. However, Shep saw a bigger picture for how they could make life more fun for people by creating unique personalized products that everyone could afford. They could change the way that the world celebrated. He was International Chairman of YPO (Young President's Organization), and today has moved to the chairman role of Shindigz. He is launching into the next chapter of his career. When I asked him why the move, he answered:

"Why do people want to launch? We realize where we are right now isn't at our full potential. If that's the search we are on, why is there a risk? If it's about being the best that we can be, then this launch is merely a step in that path towards self-actualization. That's why I don't see fear as relevant to it. It's a natural path. This isn't transactional building a business plan; this is building on who you are, who you can be and what your life means. That takes on a lot of forms of different people. You can launch into parenthood, you can launch into your career, you can launch into community service."

With this goal in mind, it's easier not to fall into a trap to pursue the traditional definitions of success. When Kate Jerome, author of a children's book series, was president of a publishing imprint under Harper Collins, others were looking at her as a role model because she was on track to become the first female CEO of a major publishing firm.

Instead of continuing along the track and fulfilling other people's pioneering aspirations for her, Kate walked away. Why? She wanted to spend more time with her young children. That's what she valued and she had to be true to that. Then, one day, National Geographic approached her. Would she be interested in writing science books for children instead? Before she was in publishing, Kate was a biology teacher.

And that's how Kate launched into her career as a children's book writer, writing 80 book series on science and geography at a time. Her books have helped hundreds of thousands of children fall in love with science. So, by being true to her values, it opened the way for new possibilities that ultimately led her to accomplish the type of positive impact she had hoped to make when she first entered into publishing.

When you understand that you are in pursuit of your best as the foundation of your launch process, you will hold yourself to a higher standard. And this can be inspiring, which in turn creates more champions.

Pat Miller, co-founder of billion-dollar brand Vera Bradley, told me about when they first started the company. If you ever meet Pat, you'll instantly get a sense of her integrity and authenticity. I still remember after I first told her about the *Thinking Cap Princesses* series, she took the time to mail me a cartoon of a dad reading a fairytale to his daughter with the note: 'And here is where the princess climbs the corporate ladder'. As busy as she was, she took time to demonstrate care.

So, it's not surprising that Vera Bradley was founded on trust and generosity. When the company began, they started with just $200, and all the vendors and workers contributed, including working for free until the bills were paid. One generous person wrote a large cheque to help them. This all happened because of deep trust and generosity. She tells me:

"People want to be inspired and to know that what they do is making a difference. They want organizations and leaders to inspire them."

Part of becoming your best self is being generous. If there's a pattern that you've picked up through this book, it's that successful launchers are also generous. By generosity, I mean that spirit of 'otherness', of thinking and acting beyond their own interests. Successful launchers are able to build their tribe and champions who are invested in their success because they also invest in other people's successes.

In short, they are also constantly paying it forward. I've had the privilege of knowing the best people in different fields: Coach K in basketball coaching; Jim Citrin in executive recruiting; Henry Friedman in neuro-oncology; Frances Hesselbein in public service; Marshall Goldsmith in executive coaching; Sim Sitkin in management; and many others who you will find throughout this book. The commonality they all share is generosity. They take the time and care to open the doors of opportunity for others. And they attract others like them.

Becoming your best you is a worthy cathedral. And if you focus on that as the end goal, it's attainable. You will focus more on the inputs into the process and hone your truest self in the process. Furthermore, what are the risks of pursuing your best you?

No need to fear. No risk.

BEHAVIOURAL ECONOMICS CONCEPT - HYBERBOLIC DISCOUNTING AND VISUALIZATION

People are very bad at thinking about and taking care of their future self. It's the notion of hyberbolic discounting. You overly discount the importance of the future for the sake of the present. That has an impact for retirement savings, what you eat, exercise.

A technique that's worked to change people's behaviour in the present is ageing software. A picture is taken and manipulated to show you how you will look in the future, say 35 years from today. You are seeing you in the future. All of a sudden, when you are able to visualize what you'll look like, you are much more of a steward for your well-being. How do you visualize the future you? The best you?

Exercise:
What's a quote that inspires you? Find a quote a day.

Create a vision board. But be sure to add things that remind you about the 'why'. For example, in my office are pictures drawn by my children. They remind me of the why behind what I do, which is to help the current generation of MBA leaders who will, in turn, create a brighter future for our children.

PART FIVE

LAUNCHING THE LAUNCH BOOK

THE INSIDE LOOK

The irony, I discovered, is that in the process of launching *The Launch Book,* and a new career path as an author, I am experiencing fear, doubts and elation. I am the readership. I am you.

In today's social media world, where what you see is everyone's highlight reels, it's easy to think about everything as easy and seamless. And you can handicap yourself by making comparisons with the lives that others lead. You compare your worst moments to what's posted, which is often the best moments – because those are the memories they want to keep and share.

Part of my hope with this book is to also share the bits of madness, the behind the scenes look at what's in my head, in my heart, as I go through the process of launching *The Launch Book*. And if I am to empower you, I need to share these with you.

I remember sending something to my friend Troy Byrd, who has helped many entrepreneurs, including helping Ray Kurzweil build Singular University, and who is a serial entrepreneur himself.

I wrote:

"Working on new outline. Will share tonight. I am a mess. But, that's ok. It's part of the process."

He wrote back:

"The best laugh I've had in a long time! I literally laughed for a minute. Because I feel your pain, I know what you're going through, and that one line represents the launch. I'm a mess (now), but it's ok (I'm thinking positive, I got this!) and it's part of the process (justifying/rationalizing your feelings or simply just recognizing where you are at in the launch process and being ok with that)."

I think it's important for you to see, to know, to believe, that it's not a smooth and seamless path. That what you feel – the ups and downs, the bits of crazy talk you tell yourself, the surges of creativity and the long spells of nothingness – that you are not alone in feeling this.

And you should not lose confidence because of the downs nor gain complacency because of the ups. These are part of the process. It's how you manage them that leads you to a meaningful, joyful, transformative outcome.

LIFE HAPPENS

T.S. Elliot may measure his life in coffee spoons. As a mom of three little ones under the age of seven, I measure my life in laundry loads, dirty dishes, meals cooked, school events and the chaos that results from the change in seasons.

I know the team at LID is wondering why they haven't heard from me. And I am grateful for their trust and faith in me. I also feel incredibly guilty, because I haven't yet committed a single word to paper.

During the day, there is the clipped pace of meetings, phone calls and work deliverables, where there are barely moments to catch one's breath. And somehow, this summer has filled up with unexpected travel – once in a lifetime, impactful and meaningful opportunities that won't always be there.

And at night, the time I've set aside to write after the kids have gone off to bed, I am exhausted. And I fall asleep. Or put my brain on automatic and catch up on all the TV shows I've missed during the week. Hulu, HBO GO, and Netflix make good bedfellows.

And there's the weekends. Those I just want to spend time with my family. Somehow, this summer and fall have filled up with events that I know will make for awesome treasured memories with my family.

Rick Wagoner, retired CEO of GM, who also had three children, once reminded me, *"The days are long, but the years are short."* And he is so right.

I want to measure my life in treasured moments, captured memories. And I am unwilling to give those up because I don't feel like I've spent meaningful time with my family during the week days. And these are things that I cannot delegate because they require care, attention and being present.

So, where do I find the time to write *The Launch Book*? Maybe I haven't found the compelling equal to that. Maybe I'm just making excuses. Maybe I'm just being really lazy.

Damn. I'm letting Martin, Nikki, and Sara at LID Publishing down.

And they are the nicest publishing team in the world, who took this leap of faith in me. I am a terrible person.

Fine. Now, what can I do to get myself moving forward? I need to build personal accountability. I need to find confidence builders. I need those who can give me the honest truth. I need to riff and test out ideas. I need to ENGAGE.

I start making a few calls.

BREAK IT DOWN

It's 18 October, the afternoon right after the Coach K Leadership Summit. We just spent two days with 25 of the most compelling leaders and leadership-thinkers in the world. Ori Brafman and I are decompressing. I told him I'm stressing out about *The Launch Book*. I don't have a single word committed on paper. In my head, the material is there. There are a gazillion different directions to take this. I am paralyzed and I need 25,000 words by eight weeks.

Ori, a member of my tribe, and a multiple time *NY Times*, best-selling author, tells me to break it down.

"Sanyin, you've written tons of 1,500 word pieces. This is just 15 of those pieces. You wrote one of those on your last visit to my house in two hours. You can do this."

You need people in your tribe to break it down for you and to remind you that you've done this before – just in a different context.

"I can do this. Thank you, Ori."

HAVE THE RIGHT FOCUS
- IT'S NOT ABOUT YOU

In my head, I've written hundreds of pages. On paper, there are only 244 words. That's 250 if you count the title and the byline. I need 25,000 words by 16 December. It's 27 October.

I write to my friend Lisa Shalett, another member of my tribe.

She emails back:

"The irony is that you are experiencing what you are writing about!! YOU are launching this book. So, pay attention to your feelings. What is uncomfortable, why, when, how you work through. Your own experience is a great guide for this – what you are going through. Ha!"

Hmmm ... this sparks an idea for what can be in the book. (Hint: you are reading it.) She writes more:

"Stop thinking about all these numbers – words, pages, whatever. Instead, remember that you are helping people with this – you are in front of students – what are the things you want to tell them, knowing it will make them smarter, more resilient, less alone-feeling. The numbers will flow from your own framing of this as contributing something generously."

She knows me. The inner circles of the members of your tribe (your lifelines), those are the people you talk to first. They know you. And because of this, she gave me a very compelling reason to get off my butt. This is me.

THE POWER OF A SINGLE ANSWER

Isabelle Wechsler, a brilliant senior whom I've known for four years, is sitting across from me. At that point in my head, I was going to recruit Isabelle to help me dive more into the research. She is also an avid reader.

She represents the potential audience for the book – interested in entrepreneurship and about to launch her career in a few months. Curious, I ask her:

"What will make you want to pick up this book? Or any book for that matter? There are tonnes of books, websites, things competing for your time."

Her answer surprised me – stories.

I know stories. I love collecting stories. There are stories in my head from the remarkable people I've spoken to. Yes, I can share those stories. These are stories that need to be amplified, many of which have not yet seen the light of day. This is who I am.

And because of this little answer, I rewrote the entire outline in a day. This book jumped into full clarity. At least for now. But I see a path forward.

Unbeknownst to Isabelle, she ignited in my heart, a little spark of hope.

IT'S GOING TO BE GREAT

I've put together an outline. I am drawing stories from my head. I'm feeling that bubbling excitement. I woke up excited to write. I couldn't wait to write. It's going to be great!

I WANT TO QUIT

This is hard. Really, wouldn't it be easier just to quit now? I would get my nights, weekends and sanity back. And only those in my inner tribe really know about the book. They won't judge if I quit now.

Ok, but what are the consequences. What would quitting say about me? My reputation with the wonderful LID team would be shot. But, they live in London. What are the chances I'll run into them again? Who am I kidding? I would feel lousy.

Why am I really writing this book? Is it ego? It seems like everyone around me is an *NY Times* best-selling author. The interesting thing about having lots of friends who are *NY Times* best-selling authors is that you get into this frame that it's normal to be on the *NY Times* best-selling list. The not so great thing about having so many *NY Times* best-selling authors for friends is that you can easily feel like a failure if your book doesn't make it on the list.

Ok, so let's draw the expectations now. I'm not looking for this to be on the *NY Times* list, and the chances are super slim. If anything, if there's to be comparison, this would probably be on the losing side in terms of numbers. The compelling reason can't be about ego. So, what's my compelling factor?

I had shared with Kristen Titus my vulnerabilities and hesitations in writing this book. Kristen is the Chief Innovation Officer for the state of New York, and formerly Executive Director of Girls Who Code. In her early thirties, she is already a wise pioneer and launcher of many great things. She tells me:

"You have a responsibility, given the expertise you have, to write this book. When you are not contributing to the world, you are missing an opportunity."

This is a meaningful consequence. And on a deeply personal level, a compelling factor is writing something that my kids would be proud of to read someday. That they may take this book off the shelf when they are launching, and it will help them.

And I'm remembering the fun in writing. There's the thrill of it, of seeing words on the page coming to life. And they may come slowly and awkwardly, but each word is one word more than what I have in the past.

I wonder if the readers are thinking me weird for having all of these inner dialogues. Kids, when you read this, just remember, it's ok to have inner dialogues and a small dose of self-doubt is not a bad thing. It's ok to be honest with yourself, confront your feelings, deal with them and find a way to move forward. Inner dialogues, drawn from reflection, are a fine tool to keep you going in the right direction.

BENDING TIME

I opened up an email first thing this morning and there's an email from Sara, my editor.

"I look forward to receiving your manuscript on 14 Dec."

Wait, 14 Dec? I thought the deadline was 16 Dec! 48 hours matter. I am panicking. My family is all ready to head out to Sunday service and I seriously contemplated skipping because would that time be better served working on the manuscript? Maybe I should skip service this morning? I decide to go.

And at Church, our pastor quoted Antoine de Saint Exupery:

"If you want to build a ship, don't drum up the men to gather wood, divide the work, and give orders. Instead, teach them to yearn for the vast and endless sea."

That is precisely what I have been looking for. *The Launch Book* is about values and mindset and, less so, about tasks. It crystallized that aspect even more. I felt lighter. No longer panicking, I went home and wrote. I wrote an entire chapter.

Sometimes, when you take time away from what you are focused on doing, you do end up creating more time and space to do exactly what you hope to accomplish.

RANDOM MOMENTS OF JOY

One day last spring, Dare Nicholson, who has the most glorious poppies in her garden, asked me: *"I saved some poppy seeds for you. Would you like me to drop them off?"*

YES. A moment of random happiness. I will capture it. It will power me through today.

RANDOM PRESENTS

The poppy seeds were beautifully packaged in a little spice jar, with a picture of what they will transform into. And the package was on my doorstep. My kids and I walk to sprinkle the seeds in our yard. They will be beautiful, salmon-coloured poppies all next spring. Isn't that something to look forward to?

This is getting metaphorical.

SEEING IS BELIEVING

I got a package from Nikki today. It's the LID Spring Catalogue. Inside, I see the picture of *The Launch Book* with a little blurb. It created a flurry of excitement and pride. I can literally see it. I believe I can do this. I just have to work backwards from that. Thank you, Nikki. You've no idea, just yet, what you've catalysed.

SOMEDAY IS TODAY

Tonight, my seven-year-old wanted to do homework with me. She peered over my shoulders to see what I was working on. I was looking at a piece I wrote – on relentless hope. On a lark, I asked her if she wanted to read it. I forgot that she might be old enough to do this. To me, she's always that little toddler. She read it out loud, slowly, tripping over words like 'virtuous' and 'inclusion'. And she caught a mistake – a repeating paragraph.

Afterwards, I asked her what it meant. She said, *"People are sad right now. But they should look up and find things to be happy about."* I love her so much.

This is why I write. I thought someday that my children could read the pieces I write, where I pour my thinking and my heart, and it might help them think and see the world differently. I didn't realize that someday is today. Tomorrow, I'm going to start letting her read *The Launch Book* in progress and get her opinions.

THE WISDOM OF STUDENTS

Caroline Blackburn, another brilliant senior and I are catching up on her fall semester. She is about to embark on a new career next fall. I run the latest outline by her. I ask her what would make her want to pick up this book?

"If it's something I think can apply to me."

I got worried. But this book isn't a 'how to' book. Also, it's not anything ground-breaking. All I hope to do is make people think and reflect.

She tells me:

"I am glad this is not a bullet list book of here's what you should do. If there was a correct list of things, obvious bullet points of 'do this,' that would have already existed. You are able to listen to other people's stories and see from your perspective and relate it to what's happening in your life. There are bits of every story that you'll be able to apply to your own life.

"It's better to look at the emotional parts of it rather than just the steps each person in the story takes. Every business is going to be different. No business is going to take the exact same steps. But everyone can relate to the frustration when you can't get something to work."

She is really helping me see why and how this can be relevant and where to focus. And affirming the necessity of the Origin Story chapter. I learn so much from the wisdom of students.

I THOUGHT IT WOULD BE EASY

I have so many stories. As I started writing them down, a glaring obstacle came into focus. Every story touches upon multiple factors in books. How am I going to structure this? I'm in so much trouble.

SERENDIPITY

I attended the celebration party of Duke Entertainment Media Arts Network (DEMAN) Weekend with my kids just to enjoy the evening. Lee Hightower, a former neighbour, introduced me to Chrislyn Choo. My children were hungry and I went to grab some food. When I returned to the table, Chrislyn and my children were engaged in a charming discussion on fictional and non-fictional stories.

Chrislyn, I discovered, is fully employed in the profession of storytelling. A neurobiologist and documentary film studies major, she is now with Story Driven, a company that helps brands tell their stories. She is the person I needed to speak with about storytelling. I was looking for neurobiological research about the biology of storytelling and why our minds are wired to process stories more readily than data. We also brainstormed over the hero's journey and she opened up her notebook to show me the most charming drawings and thoughts around the different types of stories.

I was also debating the inclusion of the parallel story in the book. Then she shared a point of view that clarified why I should:

"When we tell stories, we tend to think of ourselves as the heroes. But we should be the guide and the audience is the hero. To be an incredible guide, you need to have expertise and empathy. We are guides and the audience is coming along on their journey. And they have to come out at the end wanting to be your guide."

AMBITION STRIKES

I think I can beat the deadline.

TRUTHSAYERS

I pace in the kitchen while my husband, Chad, is reading through the 'Find Your Why' and 'Prepare for Luck' chapters.

"Well?" I asked.

"It's good. The stories are good. It's well written."

But?

"Right now, it just seems one story after another. You are not in there. You've got ideas and thoughts – bring them out. Let them see you."

He is right. I had been hiding behind stories. Wouldn't readers rather read stories about interesting people?

I ended up writing the Mentorship chapter the way I would if I were giving advice to my students.

DEADLINE MET

40,000 words in six weeks. Editing is next, which is another journey. In reality, the launch journey started before writing. For weeks, the book contract sat on my desk, unsigned. I was paralyzed with fear, for the moment I committed myself, there was the possibility of failure. I had defined failure as selling one book. And my dear husband asked me:

"If it ends up changing how that one reader thinks about their launch, if it makes them braver, and encourages them to start the process, would you consider that a success?"

"Yes," I said.

"So, make it the book that could do that, that can help the reader."

And thus, I signed the contract and started on this discovery process where I've learned so much about myself and about the others who have joined me along the way. I don't know what the outcome in terms of the traditional measures of book success will be. But I am so grateful for having gone through this journey. I hope that as you finish reading this, you feel braver and more ready to launch your own journey into the launch process.

Let's do this. You can do this. LAUNCH.

ACKNOWLEDGEMENT

The Launch Book resulted from the application of the concepts in the book. I am grateful to the tribe that helped made this a reality. Many of them are referenced in the book. Additionally, I'd like to thank my Coach K Center on Leadership & Ethics (COLE) colleagues and students - Iejumade Ajasa, Sim Sitkin, Joe LeBoeuf, Sofie Alabaster, Haley Carmichael, Jessica Womack, Mel Goetz, Krista Niemeier, McCall Wells, and Natalie Shammas; my colleagues from Dan Ariely's Duke Center for Advancement Hindsight - Susan Mettes and Kevin Brilliant; friends Alexa Gerend, RJ Lisander, Adrian Kerester, Henry Friedman, and Frank Wagner; the wonderful team at LID Publishing, especially Niki Mullins and Sara Taheri and always – my wonderful grandmother, parents, husband, and children.

ABOUT THE AUTHOR

SANYIN SIANG co-founded and leads the Coach K Center on Leadership & Ethics at Duke University's Fuqua School of Business. She is a coach and advisor to CEOs and a motivational speaker, whose advice is seen in *Forbes*, *Fortune*, and *The Wall Street Journal*. She is also an Advisor to GV (Google Ventures)